SAI SPEED MATH A

ABACUS MIND MATH

Step by Step Level – 3 Guide to Excel at Mind Math with Soroban, a Japanese Abacus

LEVEL – 3

INSTRUCTION BOOK

FOR WORKBOOKS 1 AND 2

PUBLISHED BY SAI SPEED MATH ACADEMY

USA

www.abacus-math.com

Copyright ©2015 SAI Speed Math Academy

All rights reserved. No part of this publication may be reproduced, transmitted, scanned, distributed, copied or stored in any form or by any means, electronic, mechanical, photocopying, recording, or otherwise, without prior written permission from SAI Speed Math Academy. Please do not participate in or encourage piracy of copyrighted materials which is in violation of the author's rights. Purchase only authorized editions.

Except in the United States of America, this book is sold subject to the condition that it shall not, by way of trade or otherwise, be lent, re-sold, hired out, or otherwise circulated without SAI Speed Math Academy's prior consent in any form of binding or cover other than that in which it is published and without a similar condition, including this condition being imposed on the subsequent purchaser.

Published in the United States of America by SAI Speed Math Academy, 2015

The Library of Congress has cataloged this book under this catalog number:
Library of Congress Control Number: 2014907005

ISBN of this edition: 978-1-941589-06-9

Thanks to **Abiraaman Amarnath** for his valuable contribution towards the development of this book.

Edited by: WordPlay
www.wordplaynow.com
Front Cover Image: © [Gouraud Studio] / Dollar Photo Club
www.abacus-math.com
Printed in the United States of America

Our Heartfelt Thanks to

Our

Higher Self,

Family,

Teachers,

And Friends

For the support, guidance and confidence they gave us to…

…become one of the rare people who don't know how to quit. (-Robin Sharma)

KIND REQUEST

We believe knowledge is sacred.

We believe that knowledge has to be shared.

We could have monopolized our knowledge by franchising our work and creating wealth for ourselves. However, we choose to publish books so we can reach more parents and teachers who are interested in empowering their children with mind math at a very affordable cost and with the convenience of teaching at home.

Please help us know that we made the right decision by publishing books.

- ❖ We request that you please buy our books first hand to motivate us and show us your support.
- ❖ Please do not buy used books.
- ❖ We kindly ask you to refrain from copying this book in any form.
- ❖ Help us by introducing our books to your family and friends.

We are very grateful and truly believe that we are all connected through these books. We are very grateful to all the parents who have called in or emailed us to show their appreciation and support.

Thank you for trusting us and supporting our work.

With Best Regards,

SAI Speed Math Academy

Dear Parents and Teachers,

Wonderful to see you here! Welcome to LEVEL – 3 of ABACUS MIND MATH training. We hope you had a wonderful time learning and mastering the LEVEL – 2 concepts with your students.

Thank you very much for choosing to use this LEVEL – 3 INSTRUCTION BOOK to learn, teach and excel at mind math using the Japanese abacus called the "Soroban". This is our humble effort to bring a systematic instruction manual to help introduce children to soroban. This LEVEL – 3 instruction book deals with subtraction using 10 exchange concepts also called big friends. Concepts from LEVEL – 1 and LEVEL – 2 will also be reinforced.

This book is the product of over six years of intense practice, research, and analysis of soroban. It has been perfected through learning, applying, and teaching the techniques to many students who have progressed and completed our course successfully.

We are extremely grateful to all who have been involved in this extensive process and with the development of this book.

We know that with *effort, commitment* and *tenacity*, everyone can learn to work on soroban and succeed in mind math. Just reaching LEVEL – 3 and getting ready to use this book shows that you are committed to your children's education. We are very proud to be working with you and thank you for giving us this opportunity to share our knowledge by using our books.

We wish all of you an enriching experience in learning to work on soroban and enjoying mind math excellence!

We are still learning and enjoying every minute of it!

We would like to thank you again for all your support and encouragement.

GOAL AFTER COMPLETION OF LEVEL 3 – WORKBOOKS 1 AND 2

On successful completion of the two workbooks students would be able to:
1. Subtract any two to three digit numbers that involve regrouping also known as borrowing problems.

HELPFUL SKILLS

- Must have mastered LEVEL – 1 and LEVEL – 2 concepts

PRACTICE WORKBOOKS FOR STUDENTS

There are two workbooks available for students to practice on the concepts given in this LEVEL – 3 Instruction book. Complete Workbook – 1 before proceeding to Workbook – 2. These Workbooks are **sold separately** and are available under the titles:

Abacus Mind Math Level – 3 Workbook 1 of 2 – ISBN: 978-1-941589-07-6

Abacus Mind Math Level – 3 Workbook 2 of 2 – ISBN: 978-1-941589-08-3

WE WOULD LIKE TO HEAR FROM YOU!

Please visit our Facebook page at https://www.facebook.com/AbacusMindMath. Contact us through http://www.abacus-math.com/contactus.php or email us at info@abacus-math.com

LEARNING INSTITUTIONS AND HOME SCHOOLS

If you are from any public, charter or private school, and want to provide the opportunity of learning mind math using soroban to your students, please contact us. This book is a good teaching/learning aid for small groups or for one on one class. Books for larger classrooms are set up as 'Class work books' and 'Homework books'. These books will make the teaching and learning process a smooth, successful and empowering experience for teachers and students. We can work with you to provide the best learning experience for your students.

If you are from a home school group, please contact us if you need any help.

Contents

LEVEL 3 – INSTRUCTION BOOK 1	LESSON 4 – EXAMPLE............................ 31
ATTRIBUTES TO SUCCEED 5	SAMPLE PROBLEMS 36
PLACE VALUE OF RODS 6	WEEK 5 – SPEED DICTATION 37
ORDER OF OPERATION 6	WEEK 6 – SKILL BUILDING 38
REVISION OF LEVEL 1 FORMULAS 7	WEEK 6 – SPEED DICTATION 38
REVISION OF LEVEL 2 – BIG FRIEND FORMULAS FOR ADDITION 7	WEEK 7 – LESSON 5 – INTRODUCING –7 CONCEPT 39
WEEK 1 – SUBTRACTION NUMBER SENTENCE ..8	LESSON 5 – EXAMPLE............................ 39
POINTS TO REMEMBER WHILE USING A FORMULA 11	SAMPLE PROBLEMS 41
	WEEK 7 – SPEED DICTATION 42
WEEK 2 – LESSON 1 – INTRODUCING –9 CONCEPT 14	WEEK 8 – LESSON 6 – COMPLETING –7 USING SMALL FRIENDS FORMULA 43
LESSON 1 – EXAMPLE 15	LESSON 6 – EXAMPLE............................ 44
SAMPLE PROBLEMS 17	SAMPLE PROBLEMS 49
WEEK 3 – LESSON 2 – COMPLETING –9 USING SMALL FRIENDS FORMULA 18	WEEK 8 – SPEED DICTATION 50
LESSON 2 – EXAMPLE 19	WEEK 9 – SKILL BUILDING 51
SAMPLE PROBLEMS 24	WEEK 9 – SPEED DICTATION 51
WEEK 3 – SPEED DICTATION 25	WEEK 10 – LESSON 7 – INTRODUCING –6 CONCEPT 52
WEEK 4 – LESSON 3 – INTRODUCING –8 CONCEPT 26	LESSON 7 – EXAMPLE............................ 52
LESSON 3 – EXAMPLE 26	SAMPLE PROBLEMS 54
SAMPLE PROBLEMS 28	WEEK 10 – SPEED DICTATION 55
WEEK 4 – SPEED DICTATION 29	WEEK 11 – LESSON 8 – COMPLETING –6 USING SMALL FRIENDS FORMULA 56
WEEK 5 – LESSON 4 – COMPLETING –8 USING SMALL FRIENDS FORMULA 30	LESSON 8 – EXAMPLE............................ 57
	SAMPLE PROBLEMS 62

- WEEK 11 – SPEED DICTATION 63
- WEEK 12 – LESSON 9 – INTRODUCING –5 CONCEPT 64
  - LESSON 9 – EXAMPLE 64
  - SAMPLE PROBLEMS 68
  - WEEK 12 – SPEED DICTATION 69
- WEEK 13 – LESSON 10 – INTRODUCING –4 CONCEPT 70
  - LESSON 10 – EXAMPLE 70
  - SAMPLE PROBLEMS 73
  - WEEK 13 – SPEED DICTATION 74
- WEEK 14 – LESSON 11 – INTRODUCING –3 CONCEPT 75
  - LESSON 11 – EXAMPLE 75
  - SAMPLE PROBLEMS 78
  - WEEK 14 – SPEED DICTATION 79
- WEEK 15 – LESSON 12 – INTRODUCING –2 CONCEPT 80
  - LESSON 12 – EXAMPLE 80
  - SAMPLE PROBLEMS 83
  - WEEK 15 – SPEED DICTATION 84
- WEEK 16 – LESSON 13 – INTRODUCING –1 CONCEPT 85
  - LESSON 13 – EXAMPLE 85
  - SAMPLE PROBLEMS 88
  - WEEK 16 – SPEED DICTATION 89
- WEEK 17 – LESSON 14 – BORROWING OR REGROUPING FROM HUNDREDS ROD TO SUBTRACT ON ONES ROD 90
  - LESSON 14 – EXAMPLE 91
  - LESSON 14 – SAMPLE PROBLEMS 96
  - LESSON 14 – PRACTICE PROBLEMS 97
  - WEEK 17 – SPEED DICTATION 98
- WEEK 18 – SPEED DICTATION 99
- WEEK 19 – SPEED DICTATION 100
- WEEK 20 – SPEED DICTATION 101
- WEEK 21 – SPEED DICTATION 102
- WEEK 22 – SPEED DICTATION 103
- ANSWER KEY 107

LEVEL 3 – INSTRUCTION BOOK

TOPICS COVERED

In LEVEL – 3 students will be introduced to concepts involving subtraction formulas utilizing combination facts of 10 (big friends). They will be learning formulas to subtract numbers 9 to 1. The small friend concepts learned in LEVEL – 1 and concepts from LEVEL – 2 will be extensively used in LEVEL – 3, so please make sure that the children understand all of LEVEL – 1 and LEVEL – 2 concepts before starting them on LEVEL – 3.

This instruction book helps in explaining Level – 3 concepts with example and sample problems. Practice work for this level is sold separately as Level 3 – Workbook 1 and Level 3 – Workbook 2.

Let your students use the Level 3 – Workbook 1 & 2 as you go through the lessons one by one in the order given while teaching them.
*(**Workbook 1** – has more work for the concepts found in Lesson 1 to Lesson 8.*
***Workbook 2** – has more work for the concepts found in Lesson 9 to Lesson 14.*

FINGERING

Correct fingering is very important, so practice moving earth beads and heaven beads using the correct fingers.

INSTRUCTIONS GIVEN WITHIN THE VIOLET BOX

General information to be remembered while working on the abacus is given here.

INSTRUCTIONS GIVEN WITHIN THE PINK BOX

Useful information in the process of teaching can be found in the pink box.
The most likely mistakes that a child tends to make are also explained here with ways to rectify them as needed.

Each and every child is unique in his/her own respect. His/her understanding of any new concept is also going to be vastly different. So, expect children to surprise you with unique questions and mistakes. With persistent practice, all the hurdles can be overcome.

INSTRUCTIONS GIVEN WITHIN THE RED BOX

Suggests and explains skill building activities that will help improve understanding of that particular week's concept.

SAI Speed Math Academy

BEAD COLORS

◇ = Beads that are not involved in the calculation or the game

◆ = Beads that were already in the calculation or the game

◆ = Beads that have just been moved to ADD in the game

◆ = Beads that have just been moved to MINUS from the game

The bead movements for LEVEL – 3 formulas are exact opposite to that of LEVEL – 2 formulas. Think of the formulas as out of the box thinking, or as a mind bending puzzle for kids. Here students will learn to take away more than what needs to be taken away and then put back the extra number into the game – which will be the big friend of the number they are trying to subtract. This may sound a little puzzling, however, do not be worried. Children will ease into this level within a few days.

HOW TO EXPLAIN AN EXAMPLE PROBLEM TO STUDENTS

Teachers: Practice with the example and sample problems on your abacus to become fluent with the lesson you will be introducing to your students every week.

To Teach: Use the Example problems in this Instruction Book to introduce the concept to your students.

Example 1: –34

1. Call out the number you are going to add or subtract
2. Say what you are doing on the abacus as explained in the 'Action' column of the example. Each example is explained in detail. Judge your child's maturity and skill level and explain according to their needs.

Clear	Problem	Action
Step 1	– 34	Move 3 **earth beads down** to touch the frame on the **tens rod**. Move 4 **earth beads down** to touch the frame on the **ones rod.**

Once students understand the concept:

Call out the sample problems listed and ask your students to work on their abacus or let them take turns to work on the teacher's abacus for the rest of the students to watch and follow.
OR
Work these problem on your teacher abacus and make students work on their abacus as you are calling out the numbers or to follow you as you work on your teacher's abacus.

HOW TO READ THE HAND PICTURES

While introducing subtraction fact families which requires regrouping of 10, use your hands to help children understand the relationship between numbers.

While introducing Big Friends Combination formulas (example: –9 = –10 + 1) use both of your hands to represent –10 with 10 fingers folded *(to represent subtraction of one earth bead on the tens rod)* and stretch out fingers when you add the combination friend.

Example: –9 = –10 + 1

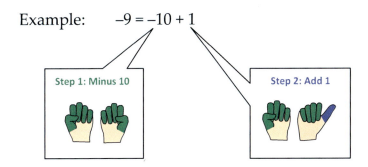

In the above example 10 is a tens place number and –10 is a moving one bead down to touch the frame on the tens place rod. The second half of the formula tells you to + 1, and one is an ones place number, and so + 1 has to be done on the ones place rod.

By using fingers, it is easy for children to memorize the fact family and also understand the big friend combination formulas. When using fingers to represent numbers, each finger is equal to 'one'. When using fingers to represent numbers adding up to 100, each finger is equal to '10'. Please do not worry that it would confuse your child because children will easily understand the concept. With practice, they will perfect their understanding.

Alternately, you may choose to use any other items like marbles, counters, beans etc. to teach.

LESSONS 1 – Introducing subtraction facts (or number sentences) of big friends combination numbers.

LESSONS 2 to 14 – Big friend subtraction formulas for –9, –8, –7, –6, –5, –4, –3, –2, –1, and borrowing or regrouping from hundreds rod to subtract on ones rod explained with examples. Each lesson has sample problems to help teachers learn and also introduce your students to a particular week's formula. Use these sample problems to teach your students before allowing them to use their corresponding workbooks.

SAI Speed Math Academy

GAMES – Some games given in the workbooks may have more than one solution. If you have a different answer than the one given in the answer key and it satisfies all the criteria, congratulations, you have a new solution.

MIND MATH – Mind math is introduced with simple problems and students who have done well with LEVEL – 1 and LEVEL – 2 mind math will be able to do these problems with ease.

If student has trouble with visualizing and computing in his/her mind, try any of the methods as explained in the LEVEL – 1 Instruction book. Do not try mind math on a challenging problem more than 3 times. If any of the methods as explained in LEVEL – 1 do not help, please do not stress students. Let them work on the abacus part of the practice work for a few days and learn the formula well. Once they are comfortable computing using the formula on the abacus, you can try going back to mind math.

Motivate and encourage them by letting them compute with only two set of numbers to begin with. A time will come when they are willing and able to do more complex mind math problems. Maintaining a nurturing attitude towards students is extremely important for success. Patience and tenacity is the key to success with mind math in this level.

The big friends subtraction concepts introduced in this level is vital for their success with division. All the formulas from LEVEL – 1 and LEVEL – 2 will be included in LEVEL – 3. So, please make sure that students understand LEVEL – 1 and LEVEL – 2 concepts very well to ensure success with LEVEL – 3.

ATTRIBUTES TO SUCCEED

ATTRIBUTE	DESCRIPTION	PARENTS/TEACHERS	CHILDREN
INTEREST	The state of wanting to know or learn about something or someone	Teaching to instill natural curiosity in children.	Learning to look to their adult teachers for guidance about the things they are curious about.
COMMITMENT	Pledge or bind (a person or an organization) to a certain course or policy	• Setting a time and place for your children every day to practice on their abacus without distractions. • Reading the instructions, and guiding and teaching until the student understands the concept.	• Learning that they are acquiring unique skills that many in their peer group do not possess. • Enthused when they understand that they are able to work out their math problems much faster without the use of calculator.
PATIENCE	The capacity to accept or tolerate delay, trouble, or suffering without getting angry or upset.	Directing children's attention back to work when they get sidetracked by TV or other distractions.	Slowly developing with consistent practice.
TENACITY	Persistent determination	"Winners never quit, quitters never win." • Teaching the value of consistent hard work with positive encouragement.	Developing the habits of persistence and hard work.
GUIDANCE	Supervised care or assistance	Providing instruction and guidance until the student learns to work independently.	Reading and understanding concepts, and ultimately working independently
REWARD	A thing given in recognition of service, effort, or achievement.	• Developing and strengthening the parent child bond by spending time together. • Teaching and enriching your child's life and learning experience.	• Learning a lifelong skill • Improving concentration • Enhancing memory power • Gaining self confidence • Developing positive self esteem

PLACE VALUE OF RODS

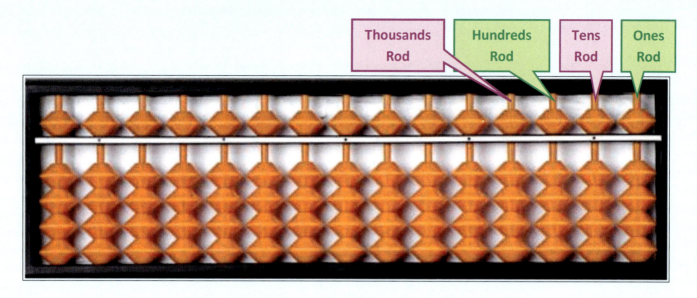

First rod from right is for the **ones place number**. All the ones place number will be set on this rod.

Second rod from right is for the **tens place number**. All the tens place number will be set on this rod.

Third rod from right is for the **hundreds place number**. All the hundreds place number will be set on this rod.

ORDER OF OPERATION

LEFT TO RIGHT: When working with two digit numbers: always add or subtract the tens place number first and then work on the ones place number.

REVISION OF LEVEL 1 FORMULAS

Small Friend Formulas for Addition and Subtractions

TO ADD	TO MINUS
+ 1 = + 5 – 4	– 1 = – 5 + 4
+ 2 = + 5 – 3	– 2 = – 5 + 3
+ 3 = + 5 – 2	– 3 = – 5 + 2
+ 4 = + 5 – 1	– 4 = – 5 + 1

REVISION OF LEVEL 2 – BIG FRIEND FORMULAS FOR ADDITION

Your child should be very familiar with the big friend combination numbers. In LEVEL – 2 children learned to use the big friend facts to achieve addition of carryover problems. In this level, they will use the big friend combination facts to achieve subtraction by regrouping or borrowing.

Big Friend Formulas for Addition

+9 = +10 – 1	+4 = +10 – 6
+8 = +10 – 2	+3 = +10 – 7
+7 = +10 – 3	+2 = +10 – 8
+6 = +10 – 4	+1 = +10 – 9
+5 = +10 – 5	+10 = +100 – 90

SAI Speed Math Academy

WEEK 1 – SUBTRACTION NUMBER SENTENCE

GOAL: For your child to know the relation between the big friend numbers and ten from a subtraction point of view.

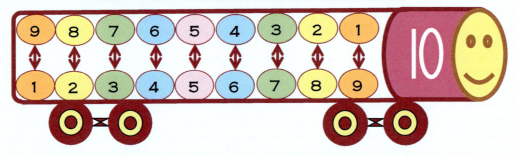

NUMBER SENTENCE FOR COMBINATIONS OF 10
Subtraction Facts

10 – 9 = 1	10 – 1 = 9
10 – 8 = 2	10 – 2 = 8
10 – 7 = 3	10 – 3 = 7
10 – 6 = 4	10 – 4 = 6
10 – 5 = 5	10 – 5 = 5

BIG FRIEND COMBINATION OF 100

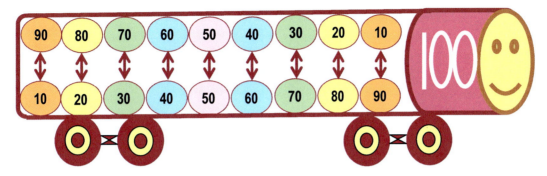

NUMBER SENTENCE FOR COMBINATIONS OF 100
Subtraction Facts

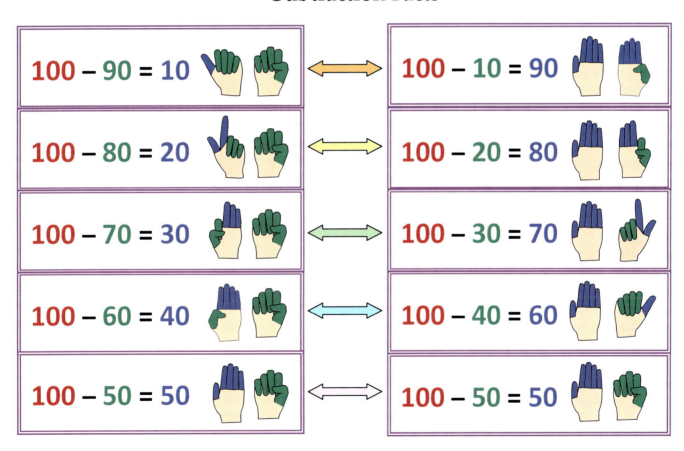

By using fingers, it is easy for children to memorize the fact family and also understand the big friend combination formulas.

SAI Speed Math Academy

EXTRA PRACTICE

- Quiz your child by asking them questions like:

    Example: 100 take away what gives 30? – Their answer should be 70

- Confuse them by asking untrue number sentences like "10 take away 5 is 6?" or "100 take away 90 is 30?" If they are clear with the combination facts their answer will be "No". Then ask them what would be the correct number sentence. As you practice, ask questions in quick succession using different number sentences.

- Quiz your child on the entire number sentence list after they complete Activity – 2 given in WORKBOOK 1 under Week – 1.

- To keep it more challenging, ask 4 to 5 number sentence questions in quick successions and ask them to give only yes or no answers. Make sure to include untrue number sentences in the question list. You may also choose the activity suggested in the first bullet point here for this rapid round quiz.

- Students will have to be very attentive hearing your questions and coming up with answers which will improve their presence of mind and concentration.

- Most importantly, make it fun for your children to participate and learn.

POINTS TO REMEMBER WHILE USING A FORMULA

In this level, students will learn to use big friend combination facts to achieve subtraction (minus) by regrouping or borrowing from a bigger place value number/rod.

In LEVEL 2, children learned to add by adding at a higher place value rod and removing the big friend of the number they are trying to add on their working rod.

In LEVEL 3, they will learn to subtract a number by subtracting at a higher place value rod and adding the excess onto their working rod. The excess would be the big friend of the number they are trying to subtract.

Think of the formulas as out of the box, mind bending puzzles for kids. LEVEL – 3 formulas may seem like they would be challenging to teach young children, but do not be worried; children will ease into this level with a few days of practice.

1. **Use the formula only when you do not have enough beads to subtract.**
   When you teach a formula, most kids understand and remember this fact. However, some children will try to do the formula even when they can directly subtract a number. They will do –10 and get confused about why they do not have enough beads to add the big friend of the number they are computing on the working rod. So, care has to be taken to make students understand that formulas are to be used **only** when they do not have enough beads to compute.

2. **When formula is introduced, ask students to –10** (or –100) **first and then add the corresponding big friend of the number they are trying to subtract from the game onto the working rod.**

    a) **You can present the formula in a cohesive order for students to follow.**

    Condition: Students have to subtract a number but do not have enough beads on the working rod.

    We know that 10 (or 100) has the number we are trying to subtract. So let us make use of this fact by doing – 10 (or –100). Now, we have taken out more than what we should have from the game. So, to make it right, we have to add the big friend of the number we are trying to subtract back into the game.

    Example: 15 – 9
    Ones rod has the heaven bead in the game; however, its value is 5 which is not going to be enough. Now, we know that 9 cannot be subtracted directly.

The next option we have is the ten bead.
We know that the 10 bead has a nine in it (9 + 1 = 10)
so, we need to get help from 10 by sending it out of the game.
- Subtract 10 from the game.

We know that 10 is 1 more than 9.
So, to keep 9 out of the game, we have to put 1 back into the game.
- Add 1 to the working rod.

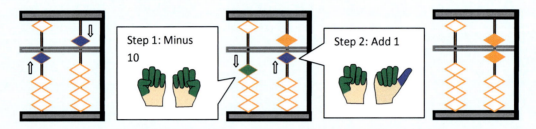

Big friend formulas for subtracting are easier to remember this way rather than just asking students to add friend and then take out one bead on the rod to the left – the general way formulas are taught. Students can be taught to follow general method too, but make sure that they understand why they are adding the friend and subtracting one bead on the rod to the left.

b) Subtracting 10 or 100 and then adding the big friend will bring students back to the rod they are working.

When you follow the formula in the order given, students will come back to the same rod they are working on and it is easy for them to move on to the next place value to continue computing.

Example: 104 – 93 = 11

When using the formula to do –90 (9 here is a tens place number), first –100 and then +10. Now, by following this order, their finger is back on the tens place rod and they have to move to the ones place rod to –3.

If students follow the general method, they first add the friend on the tens rod (working rod) and then –100, which leaves their finger on the hundreds rod. The next number to compute is –3 for which they have to consciously skip the tens place rod and go to ones place rod. Young students will be challenged in remembering to skip the tens rod and move to ones place rod to finish computing. But like anything, with practice students may overcome this hurdle. Choose the method you think best fits your students' ability to understand and follow the formulas.

3. **Visual Aid –** As a visual aid show them both hands with fingers folded to represent –10 (or –100), and then outstretch the fingers to represent adding of the corresponding big friend. By this *(the folded fingers represent the subtracted number)* they can visually see how following the formula helps them subtract a number indirectly (out of the box thinking).

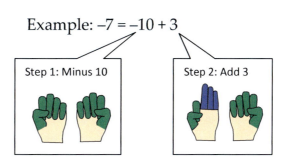

4. **Encourage them to use the reason and figure out the formulas on their own.**

   After students understand the pattern (s/he will have to be taught a few formulas to get to this point) encourage them to figure out the rest of the big friend formulas on their own. Most students are very eager to guess the next formula and explain the reason as to why the formula works.

5. **This in turn encourages them to stay motivated and increases their self confidence.**

ATTENTION
- "Bead is in the game" = adding
- "Bead is out of the game" = subtracting
- "Working rod" = the rod on which you are trying to add or subtract that corresponds to the place value of the number you are computing.

WEEK 2 – LESSON 1 – INTRODUCING –9 CONCEPT

1) Always set abacus to zero by clearing all the beads away from the beam before starting each calculation.

2) Setting numbers on the abacus:

      Hundreds place numbers go on the hundreds rod.

      Tens place numbers go on the tens rod.

      Ones place numbers go on the ones rod.

LESSON 1 – EXAMPLE

CONCEPTS OF THE WEEK

TO MINUS = MINUS 10, ADD BIG FRIEND $-9 = -10 + 1$ $-90 = -100 + 10$

EXAMPLE: 1

1	After	+ 30	- 09 (-10 +1)	= 21
30 - 09 21	ABACUS LOOKS LIKE	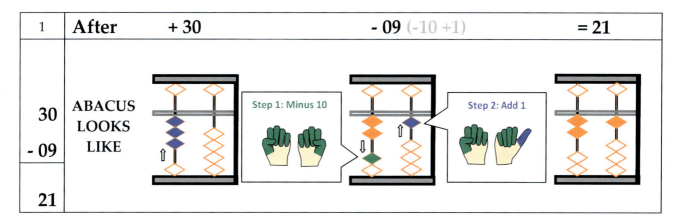		

Problem	Action
+ 30	Move **three earth beads** to touch the beam on the **tens rod.** There is nothing to do on the ones rod because ones place number is zero.
- 09	There is nothing to do on the tens rod because tens place number is zero. Now we need to –9 on the ones rod, but we do not have enough beads on the ones rod to do –9. So, now we need to make use of the fact that **10 = 9 + 1.** **When you want to –9 and you do not have enough beads:** Use $-9 = -10 +1$ Big Friend formula to do your calculations. Step 1: Minus 10 – Move **one earth bead down** to touch the frame on the **tens rod.** *(One earth bead on the tens rod is equal to '10')* *We know that there is a nine in the ten (9 + 1 = 10), so let us get help from 10 by sending it away from our game. However, we were supposed to –9, instead we did –10, which means we have sent 1 more than what we should have sent away. So, now we have to bring the 1 back into our game.* Step 2: Add 1 – Move **one earth bead up** to touch the beam on the **ones rod.** *(When we do –10 and +1, we get to keep 9 out of our game.)* $\boxed{-10 +1 = -9}$

EXAMPLE: 2   − 90 = − 100 + 10

1	+260	(-100 + 10) - 90	= 170
260 - 90 170		Step 1: Minus 100 Step 2: Add 10	

Problem	Action
+ 260	Set the numbers on their appropriate place value rods.
- 90	Now we need to −90 on the tens rod, but we do not have enough earth beads to do −90 on the tens rod. So, now we need to make use of the fact that **100 = 90 + 10**. **When you want to −90 and you do not have enough beads:** **Use −90 = −100 +10 Big Friend formula to do your calculations.** *(This can be taught as using the same bead movement as for −9, however minus on the hundreds rod and add on the tens rod.)* <u>Step 1: Minus 100</u> – Move **one earth bead down** to touch the frame on the **hundreds rod**. <u>Step 2: Add 10</u> – Move **one earth bead up** to the beam on the **tens rod**. There is nothing to do on the ones rod because ones place number is zero.

ATTENTION

- Ask students to say the formula while they use it. This makes it easy for them to understand and follow through with all the steps in the formula. This will help with their presence of mind and avoid confusion.
- Students are used to adding on the higher place value rod and subtracting on the working rod. Now, they may do −10 to follow this level's formula. However, instead of +1 they may do −1 (which is second half of the +9 formula) due to force of habit.
- When subtracting 19 (where they need to use the −9 formula) students will −10 once and then +1. Make sure they understand that they have to -10 once for the ten in the 19 and **another** −10 to use the formula before finishing with +1 while doing −9. E.g., 31 − 19
- When following the formula on the tens rod, students usually −100 but then get confused and try to do +1 instead of +10. Make them understand that big friend of 90 is 10 and they help each other.

SAMPLE PROBLEMS

TO INTRODUCE –9 = – 10 + 1 FORMULA

Work with these problems a few times to study and understand the concept and the relationship between the beads moved.

1	2	3	4	5	6	7	8	9	10
19	22	38	42	57	50	65	44	56	87
- 09	- 09	- 09	- 19	- 19	- 19	- 29	11	- 14	- 34
- 09	- 09	- 09	- 09	- 19	- 19	- 29	- 19	- 39	- 19

TO INTRODUCE –90 = – 100 + 10 FORMULA

Work with these problems a few times to study and understand the concept and the relationship between the beads moved.

1	2	3	4	5	6	7	8	9	10
64	28	99	68	58	117	176	288	421	508
70	93	06	35	44	- 09	- 90	- 99	- 19	- 199
- 91	- 99	- 99	- 90	- 90	- 94	- 09	- 99	- 190	- 99

1	2	3	4	5	6	7	8	9	10
59	87	48	95	86	97	88	155	502	601
19	45	56	25	34	26	55	15	- 190	370
- 36	- 91	15	35	- 99	- 19	68	76	- 190	- 149
- 29	- 39	- 99	- 91	- 19	- 91	- 199	- 19	- 19	- 490

POINTS TO REMEMBER

The rows above consist of sample problems to introduce this week's formula. Explain to your child when and how to use the formula. Work with the sample problems until your child understands the formula and that the formulas are to be used ONLY when there are not enough beads to add or subtract.

WEEK 3 – LESSON 2 – COMPLETING –9 USING SMALL FRIENDS FORMULA

CONCEPTS OF THE WEEK

TO MINUS = MINUS 10, ADD BIG FRIEND   – 9 = – 10 + 1   – 90 = – 100 + 10

– 9 = – 10 + 1   – 90 = – 100 + 10
GET HELP FROM   **GET HELP FROM**
–10 = –50 +40   –100 = –500 +400
+1 = +5 –4   +10 = +50 –40

By now, students should be at ease working with the –9 formula. In the previous lesson, all the problems where they had to use the formula were simple and students were able to follow the –9 formula directly. This week, they will learn to get help from our LEVEL–1 Small Friends formula of –10 and +1 in order to complete –9 formula. Students will understand this week's concept if you make them understand that they are "getting help" from LEVEL 1 formulas to do –9. You may choose to give a review quiz/dictation on lessons nine and ten in LEVEL 1 before introducing them to this week's lesson.

Example 1:   56 – 9 = 47
Set 56 on the abacus. Now to –9, we need to follow the formula of **–9 = –10 + 1**, but we cannot do –10 directly. So to do –10, you have to follow **–10 = –50 +40** formula from LEVEL – 1.

Example 2:   14 – 09 = 05
Set 14 on the abacus. Now to –9, we need to follow the formula of **–9 = –10 +1**. Here, you can directly do –10 however, you do not have enough ones bead on the ones rod to do +1. So to do +1, you get help from the **+1 = +5 – 4** formula from LEVEL – 1.

Example 3:   54 – 09 = 45
Set 54 on the abacus. Here too we need to use the **–9 = –10 +1** formula. However, both –10 and +1 cannot be done directly. To do both these steps, you have to get help from LEVEL – 1 Small Friends formulas for **–10 = –50 +40** and **+1 = +5 –4**.

Example 4:   240 – 90 = 150
Set 240 on the abacus. To do –90, we now need to use the formula **–90 = –100 +10**. Here, to complete the steps you will have to get help from LEVEL – 1 Small Friends formulas for **+10 = +50 –40**.

LESSON 2 – EXAMPLE

EXAMPLE: 1

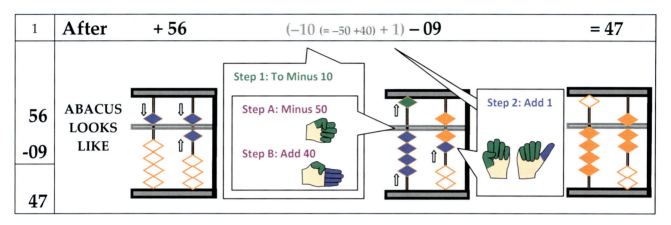

1	After	+ 56	(–10 (= –50 +40) + 1) – 09		= 47

56
-09
47

Problem	Action
+ 56	Set the numbers on their appropriate place value rods.
– 09	There is nothing to do on the tens rod because the tens place number is zero. Now we need to –9 on the ones rod, but we do not have enough beads on the ones rod to do –9. *(The heaven bead is in the game, but it does not have nine in it, so we cannot get help from it.)* So, now we need to make use of the fact that **10 = 9 + 1.** **When you want to –9 and you do not have enough beads:** **Use –9 = –10 +1 Big Friend formula to do your calculations.** *Now to do –10 you do not have enough earth beads so, GET HELP from small friend formula and do –10.* <u>Step 1: Minus 10 =</u> <u>Step A: Minus 50</u> – Move the heaven bead up to touch the frame on the tens rod. <u>Step B: Adds 40</u> – Move all four earth beads up to touch the beam on the tens rod. **Now complete the –9 formula by doing +1 on the ones rod.** <u>Step 2: Add 1</u> – Move **one earth bead up** to touch the beam on the **ones rod**. *(When we do –10 and +1, we get to keep 9 out of our game.)* $\boxed{-10 +1 = -9}$

SAI Speed Math Academy

EXAMPLE: 2

| 1 | + 14 | (−10 +1(= +5 − 4)) − 09 | = 05 |

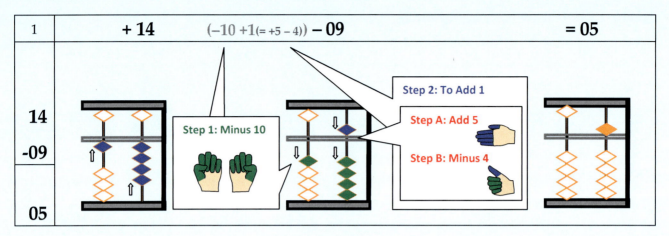

Problem	Action
+ 14	Set the numbers on their appropriate place value rods.

− 09	There is nothing to do on the tens rod because the tens place number is zero.
	
	Now we need to −9 on the ones rod, but we do not have enough beads on the ones rod to do −9. So, now we need to make use of the fact that **10 = 9 + 1.**
	
	When you want to −9 and you do not have enough beads:
	Use −9 = −10 +1 Big Friend formula to do your calculations.
	Step 1: Minus 10 – Move **one earth bead down** to touch the frame on the **tens rod.**
	(One earth bead on the tens rod is equal to '10')
	
	Now we need to finish the formula by doing +1 on the ones rod, but we do not have earth beads to do +1 so, GET HELP from small friend formula and do +1.
	Step 2: Add 1 =
	  Step A: Add 5 – Move the heaven bead down to touch the beam on the ones rod.
	  Step B: Minus 4 – Move all four earth beads down to touch the frame on the ones rod.
	
	(When we do −10 and +1, we get to keep 9 out of our game.)
	
	          − 10 +1 = − 9

EXAMPLE: 3

1	+ 54	− 09 (−10 (= −50 + 40) +1(= +5 − 4))	= 45
54 -09 45	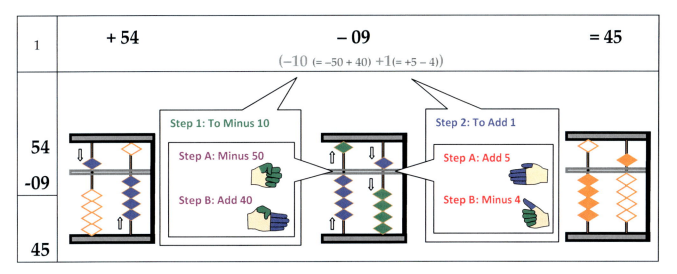		

Problem	Action
+ 54	Set the numbers on their appropriate place value rods.

− 09	There is nothing to do on the tens rod because the tens place number is zero.
	
	Now we need to −9 on the ones rod, but we do not have enough beads on the ones rod to do −9. So, now we need to make use of the fact that **10 = 9 + 1.**
	
	When you want to −9 and you do not have enough beads:
	Use −9 = −10 +1 Big Friend formula to do your calculations.
	Now to do −10 you do not have enough beads so, GET HELP from small friend formula and do −10.
	Step 1: Minus 10 =
	   Step A: Minus 50 – Move the heaven bead up to touch the frame on the tens rod.
	   Step B: Adds 40 – Move all four earth beads up to touch the beam on the tens rod.
	
	Now we need to finish the formula by doing +1 on the ones rod, but we do not have enough earth beads to do +1 so, GET HELP from small friend formula and do +1.
	Step 2: Add 1 =
	   Step A: Add 5 – Move the heaven bead down to touch the beam on the ones rod.
	   Step B: Minus 4 – Move all four earth beads down to touch the frame on the ones rod.
	
	(When we do −10 and +1, we get to keep 9 out of our game.)
	
	$\boxed{-10 +1 = -9}$

EXAMPLE: 4

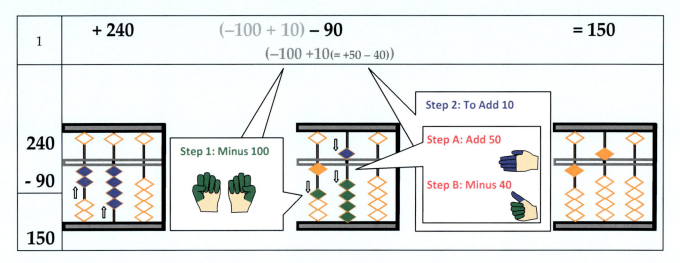

| 1 | + 240 | (−100 + 10) − 90
(−100 +10(= +50 − 40)) | = 150 |

Problem	Action
+ 240	Set the numbers on their appropriate place value rods.

−90	Now we need to −90 on the tens rod, but we do not have enough earth beads to do −90 on the tens rod. So, now we need to make use of the fact that **100 = 90 + 10**.
	When you want to −90 and you do not have enough beads:
	Use **−90 = −100 + 10 Big Friend formula to do your calculations.**
	(This can be taught as using the same bead movement as for −9, but minus on the hundreds rod and add on the tens rod.)
	Step 1: Minus 100 – Move **one earth bead down** to touch the frame on the **hundreds rod.**
	Now we need to finish the formula by doing + 10 on the tens rod, but we do not have enough earth bead to do +10 so, GET HELP from small friends formula and do + 10.
	Step 2: Add 10 =
	  Step A: Add 50 – Move the heaven bead down to touch the beam on the tens rod.
	  Step B: Minus 40 – Move all four earth beads down to touch the frame on the tens rod.
	There is nothing to do on the ones rod because the ones place number is zero
	(When we do −100 and +10, we get to keep 90 out of our game.)

ATTENTION

- Ask students to say the formula while they use it. This makes it easy for them to understand and follow through with all the steps in the formula.
- **Do not** say the small friend formula even when you are getting help from it. For instance, in example 4, JUST SAY "+ 10" while performing the small friend formula bead movements. Do not say the small friend formula out loud.

EXAMPLE: 5 $-90 = -100 + 10$

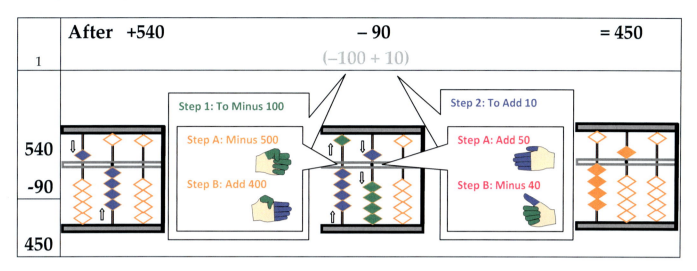

Problem	Action
+ 540	Set the numbers on their appropriate place value rods.
– 90	Now we need to –90 on the tens rod, but we do not have enough beads on the tens rod to do –90. So, now we need to make use of the fact that **100 = 90 + 10**. **When you want to –90 and you do not have enough beads:** **Use –90 = –100 + 10 Big Friend formula to do your calculations.** *Now to do –100 you do not have enough beads so, GET HELP from small friend formula and do –100.* <u>Step 1: Minus 100 =</u> <u>Step A: Minus 500</u> – Move the heaven bead up to touch the frame on the hundreds rod. <u>Step B: Add 400</u> – Move all four earth beads up to touch the beam on the hundreds rod. *Now we need to finish the formula by doing +10 on the tens rod, but we do not have enough earth beads to do +10 so, GET HELP from small friend formula and do +10.* <u>Step 2: Add 10 =</u> <u>Step A: Add 50</u> – Move the heaven bead down to touch the beam on the tens rod. <u>Step B: Minus 40</u> – Move all four earth beads down to touch the frame on the tens rod. *(When we do –100 and +10, we get to keep 90 out of our game.)* $\boxed{-100 + 10 = -90}$ There is nothing to do on the ones rod because the ones place number is zero.

SAI Speed Math Academy

SAMPLE PROBLEMS

$$-9 = -10 + 1 \qquad\qquad -90 = -100 + 10$$

TO INTRODUCE +1 OR +10 BY GETTING HELP FROM SMALL FRIENDS
FORMULA OF +1 = +5 –4 OR +10 = +50 –40

Work these problems a few times to study and understand the concept and the relationship between the beads moved.

1	2	3	4	5	6	7	8	9	10
44	23	53	55	43	114	142	174	143	263
01	- 09	- 19	- 11	- 09	- 90	- 90	- 39	- 90	- 29
10	- 09	- 09	- 19	- 19	- 09	- 19	- 90	- 19	- 99

3:S:1 © SAI Speed Math Academy, USA

TO INTRODUCE –10 OR –100 BY GETTING HELP FROM SMALL FRIENDS
FORMULA OF –10 = –50 +40 OR –100 = –500 +400

Work these problems a few times to study and understand the concept and the relationship between the beads moved.

1	2	3	4	5	6	7	8	9	10
55	52	56	64	55	530	665	563	154	544
- 11	- 09	- 09	- 19	- 01	- 90	- 219	- 99	- 09	- 90
	- 09	- 19	- 09	- 09	- 90	- 90	- 29	- 90	- 09

3:S:2 © SAI Speed Math Academy, USA

1	2	3	4	5	6	7	8	9	10
93	74	17	44	36	34	46	147	263	159
- 09	- 09	89	74	08	70	88	- 93	- 19	35
- 09	- 19	- 90	- 09	- 09	- 99	- 99	- 19	- 99	- 49

3:S:3 © SAI Speed Math Academy, USA

POINTS TO REMEMBER

The rows above consist of sample problems to introduce this week's formula. Explain to your child when and how to use the formula. Work with the sample problems until your child understands the formula and that the formulas are to be used ONLY when there are not enough beads to add or subtract.

WEEK 3 – SPEED DICTATION

Goal with speed dictation is to be able to increase the speed of child's calculating skill. For example, if you are dictating 5 numbers in 10 to 15 seconds, slowly increase your dictating speed by giving more numbers in the same time. Try to reach dictating 10 numbers in 10 to 15 seconds. With patience and practice everyone will be able to reach this goal. Most important is that you keep this exercise a fun activity for kids. Start with dictating 3 to 4 numbers and then slowly add more numbers till students can comfortably calculate all the numbers given in each row in mind. Students will develop more focus and a presence of mind with continued practice of this activity.

1	2	3	4	5	6	7	8	9	10
01	02	06	08	03	04	03	07	05	05
01	01	02	01	03	02	01	- 02	01	02
02	02	- 03	- 05	- 01	- 01	03	- 02	- 04	- 03
01	- 04	- 03	01	- 01	- 02	01	01	05	04
- 02	03	05	- 02	04	05	- 04	02	- 03	01
03	05	- 04	03	- 02	- 03	01	- 04	01	- 07
- 04	- 06	02	- 04	- 02	01	- 02	03	- 02	04
05	02	01	02	05	- 04	05	- 02	03	- 02
- 03	02	- 05	02	- 08	02	- 01	05	- 01	05
01	- 04	04	- 06	06	02	- 03	- 07	- 01	- 06

1	2	3	4	5	6	7	8	9	10
30	60	90	40	20	40	50	70	10	80
10	- 40	- 60	40	20	30	10	10	40	- 20
10	50	50	10	20	10	- 40	- 30	- 10	- 20
10	- 30	- 70	- 70	20	- 20	50	20	20	- 30
- 40	10	60	30	- 30	- 10	- 30	- 40	- 30	50
20	- 20	20	10	- 40	40	10	20	60	- 40
20	50	- 80	- 20	30	- 80	20	- 10	- 80	30
20	- 40	40	10	30	40	- 40	50	40	30
- 60	10	- 10	40	- 20	20	50	- 70	- 20	- 60
10	- 50	50	- 60	- 20	- 30	- 60	- 10	50	40

SAI Speed Math Academy

WEEK 4 – LESSON 3 – INTRODUCING –8 CONCEPT

LESSON 3 – EXAMPLE

CONCEPTS OF THE WEEK

TO MINUS = MINUS 10, ADD BIG FRIEND $-8 = -10 + 2$ $-80 = -100 + 20$

EXAMPLE: 1

1	**After**	**+ 40**	**- 08** (-10 +2)	**= 32**
40 - 08 32	ABACUS LOOKS LIKE		Step 1: Minus 10 — Step 2: Add 2	

Problem	Action
+ 40	Move **four earth beads** to touch the beam on the **tens rod**. There is nothing to do on the ones rod because ones place number is zero.
- 08	There is nothing to do on the tens rod because tens place number is zero. Now we need to –8 on the ones rod, but we do not have enough beads on the ones rod to do –8. So, now we need to make use of the fact that **10 = 8 + 2**. **When you want to –8 and you do not have enough beads:** Use **–8 = – 10 + 2** Big Friend formula to do your calculations. Step 1: Minus 10 – Move **one earth bead down** to touch the frame on the **tens rod**. *(One earth bead on the tens rod is equal to '10')* *We know that there is a eight in the ten (8 + 2 = 10), so let us get help from 10 by sending it away from our game. However, we were supposed to –8, instead we did –10, which means we have sent 2 more than what we should have sent away. So, now we have to bring the 2 back into our game.* Step 2: Add 2 – Move **two earth beads up** to touch the beam on the **ones rod**. *(When we do –10 and +2, we get to keep 8 out of our game.)* $- 10 + 2 = - 8$

EXAMPLE: 2 $-80 = -100 + 20$

1	+170	(-100 + 20) - 80	= 90
170 - 80 90			

Problem	Action
+ 170	Set the numbers on their appropriate place value rods.
- 80	Now we need to –80 on the tens rod, but we do not have enough earth beads to do –80 on the tens rod. So, now we need to make use of the fact that **100 = 80 + 20**. **When you want to –80 and you do not have enough beads:** Use **–80 = –100 +20** Big Friend formula to do your calculations. *(This can be taught as using the same bead movement as for –8, however minus on the hundreds rod and add on the tens rod.)* <u>Step 1: Minus 100</u> – Move **one earth bead down** to touch the frame on the **hundreds rod**. <u>Step 2: Add 20</u> – Move **two earth beads up** to the beam on the **tens rod**. There is nothing to do on the ones rod because ones place number is zero.

ATTENTION

- Ask students to say the formula while they use it. This makes it easy for them to understand and follow through with all the steps in the formula. This will help with their presence of mind and avoid confusion.
- Students are used to adding on the higher place value rod and subtracting on the working rod. Now, they may do –10 to follow this level's formula. However, instead of +2 they may do **–2** (which is second half of the +9 formula) due to force of habit.
- When subtracting 18 (where they need to use the –8 formula) students will –10 once and then +2. Make sure they understand that they have to -10 once for the ten in the 18 and **another** –10 to use the formula before finishing with +2 while doing –8. E.g., 31 – 18
- When following the formula on the tens rod, students usually –100 but then get confused and try to do +2 instead of +20. Make them understand that big friend of 80 is 20 and they help each other.

SAI Speed Math Academy

SAMPLE PROBLEMS

TO INTRODUCE −8 = −10 + 2 FORMULA

Work with these problems a few times to study and understand the concept and the relationship between the beads moved.

1	2	3	4	5	6	7	8	9	10
18	20	39	35	57	50	65	33	55	77
- 08	- 08	- 08	- 18	- 18	- 18	- 28	22	- 13	- 18
- 08	- 08	- 08	- 08	- 18	- 18	- 28	- 18	- 18	- 18

TO INTRODUCE −80 = −100 + 20 FORMULA

Work with these problems a few times to study and understand the concept and the relationship between the beads moved.

1	2	3	4	5	6	7	8	9	10
50	66	177	125	158	121	170	279	337	560
50	60	- 80	- 80	- 88	- 80	- 80	- 88	- 18	- 188
- 80	- 88	- 88	- 18	- 18	- 18	- 88	- 88	- 188	- 188

1	2	3	4	5	6	7	8	9	10
75	66	63	75	88	82	49	63	194	273
68	95	15	49	57	84	- 18	28	117	157
- 92	- 89	24	17	- 19	- 59	- 18	44	- 88	- 18
- 18	33	- 89	- 18	- 18	- 81	88	- 18	- 89	- 91

POINTS TO REMEMBER

The rows above consist of sample problems to introduce this week's formula. Explain to your child when and how to use the formula. Work with the sample problems until your child understands the formula and that the formulas are to be used ONLY when there are not enough beads to add or subtract.

WEEK 4 – SPEED DICTATION

Goal with speed dictation is to be able to increase the speed of child's calculating skill. Start with dictating 5 sets of numbers in 10 to 15 seconds and slowly increase giving more numbers in the same time.

1	2	3	4	5	6	7	8	9	10
22	44	11	33	66	55	44	11	77	88
22	22	11	11	11	22	11	55	22	- 55
11	- 33	44	- 22	- 22	22	- 22	- 22	- 66	22
22	55	- 22	55	- 33	- 77	55	11	22	- 33
- 33	- 44	33	- 33	- 11	44	- 44	- 44	- 11	- 11
44	11	- 22	44	44	33	22	33	55	44
- 55	- 22	- 11	- 33	22	- 88	- 33	22	- 77	- 22
22	33	55	- 22	- 44	33	11	- 33	44	55
- 11	- 22	- 66	11	22	11	22	55	- 33	- 66
33	- 44	22	11	- 33	- 22	22	- 88	- 33	77

1	2	3	4	5	6	7	8	9	10
55	77	22	88	33	55	99	44	22	44
11	- 44	44	- 66	11	44	- 55	44	55	33
- 44	- 11	33	33	22	- 77	33	- 33	- 11	11
55	22	- 22	- 11	33	33	- 66	22	- 44	- 22
- 33	22	- 11	- 11	- 44	- 22	44	- 11	22	- 11
11	- 11	- 33	22	22	11	- 22	22	11	- 44
22	- 11	22	33	- 66	44	44	- 11	- 22	33
- 44	- 22	44	- 77	22	- 66	11	22	55	22
55	66	- 77	44	11	- 11	- 22	- 55	- 11	- 33
11	- 44	66	22	11	22	- 22	11	- 44	- 22

SAI Speed Math Academy

WEEK 5 – LESSON 4 – COMPLETING –8 USING SMALL FRIENDS FORMULA

CONCEPTS OF THE WEEK
TO MINUS = MINUS 10, ADD BIG FRIEND   – 8 = – 10 + 2   – 80 = – 100 + 20
– 8 = – 10 + 2   – 80 = – 100 + 20
GET HELP FROM   **GET HELP FROM**
–10 = –50 +40   –100 = –500 +400
+2 = +5 –3   +20 = +50 –30

By now, students should be at ease working with the –8 formula. In the previous lesson, all the problems where they had to use the formula were simple and students were able to follow the –8 formula directly. This week, they will learn to get help from our LEVEL–1 Small Friends formula of –10 and +2 in order to complete –8 formula. Students will understand this week's concept if you make them understand that they are "getting help" from LEVEL 1 formulas to do –8. You may choose to give a review quiz/dictation on lessons ten and eleven in LEVEL 1 before introducing them to this week's lesson.

Example 1:   57 – 8 = 49

Set 57 on the abacus. Now to –8, we need to follow the formula of –**8**= –**10** + **2**, but we cannot do –10 directly. So to do –10, you have to follow –10 = –50 +40 formula from LEVEL – 1.

Example 2:   33 – 08 = 25

Set 33 on the abacus. Now to –8, we need to follow the formula of –**8** = –**10** +**2**. Here, you can directly do –10 however, you do not have enough ones bead on the ones rod to do +2. So to do +2, you get help from the +2 = +5 – 3 formula from LEVEL – 1.

Example 3:   54 – 08 = 46

Set 54 on the abacus. Here too we need to use the –**8** = –**10** +**2** formula. However, both –10 and +2 cannot be done directly. To do both these steps, you have to get help from LEVEL – 1 Small Friends formulas for –10 = –50 +40 **and** +2 = +5 –3.

Example 4:   130 – 80 = 50

Set 130 on the abacus. To do –80, we now need to use the formula –**80** = –**100** +**20**. Here, to complete the steps you will have to get help from LEVEL – 1 Small Friends formulas for +20 = +50 –30.

LESSON 4 – EXAMPLE

EXAMPLE: 1

1	After	+ 57	(–10 (= –50 +40) + 2) – 08	= 49

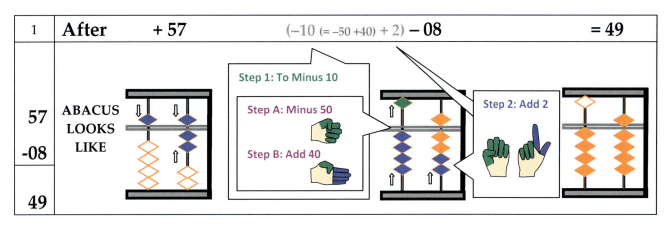

57	ABACUS LOOKS LIKE
-08	
49	

Problem	Action
+ 57	Set the numbers on their appropriate place value rods.

– 08	There is nothing to do on the tens rod because the tens place number is zero.
	
	Now we need to –8 on the ones rod, but we do not have enough beads on the ones rod to do –8. *(The heaven bead is in the game, but it does not have eight in it, so we cannot get help from it.)* So, now we need to make use of the fact that **10 = 8 + 2**.
	
	When you want to –8 and you do not have enough beads:
	Use –8 = –10 + 2 Big Friend formula to do your calculations.
	Now to do –10 you do not have enough earth beads so, GET HELP from small friend formula and do –10.
	Step 1: Minus 10 =
	  Step A: Minus 50 – Move the heaven bead up to touch the frame on the tens rod.
	  Step B: Adds 40 – Move all four earth beads up to touch the beam on the tens rod.
	
	Now complete the –8 formula by doing +2 on the ones rod.
	  Step 2: Add 2 – Move **two earth beads up** to touch the beam on the **ones rod**.
	
	(When we do –10 and +2, we get to keep 8 out of our game.)
	
	$$-10 + 2 = -8$$

SAI Speed Math Academy   Pg 31

EXAMPLE: 2

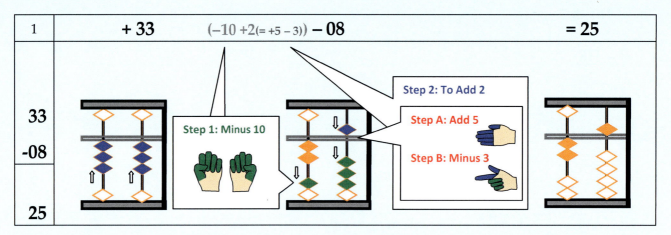

Problem	Action
+ 33	Set the numbers on their appropriate place value rods.
– 08	There is nothing to do on the tens rod because the tens place number is zero. Now we need to –8 on the ones rod, but we do not have enough beads on the ones rod to do –8. So, now we need to make use of the fact that **10 = 8 + 2.** **When you want to –8 and you do not have enough beads:** Use **–8 = –10 +2** Big Friend formula to do your calculations. <u>Step 1: Minus 10</u> – Move **one earth bead down** to touch the frame on the **tens rod.** *(One earth bead on the tens rod is equal to '10')* Now we need to finish the formula by doing +2 on the ones rod, but we do not have earth beads to do +2 so, GET HELP from small friend formula and do +2. <u>Step 2: Add 2</u> = <u>Step A: Add 5</u> – Move the heaven bead down to touch the beam on the ones rod. <u>Step B: Minus 3</u> – Move three earth beads down to touch the frame on the ones rod. *(When we do –10 and +2, we get to keep 8 out of our game.)* – 10 +2 = – 8

EXAMPLE: 3

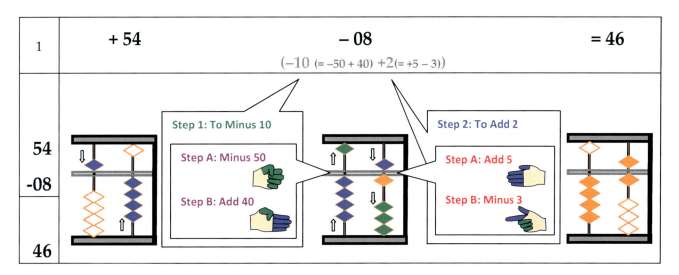

1	+ 54	− 08	= 46
		(−10 (= −50 + 40) +2 (= +5 − 3))	

Problem	Action
+ 54	Set the numbers on their appropriate place value rods.

− 08	There is nothing to do on the tens rod because the tens place number is zero.
	
	Now we need to −8 on the ones rod, but we do not have enough beads on the ones rod to do −8. So, now we need to make use of the fact that **10 = 8 + 2.**
	
	When you want to −8 and you do not have enough beads:
	Use −8 = −10 +2 Big Friend formula to do your calculations.
	Now to do −10 you do not have enough beads so, GET HELP from small friend formula and do −10.
	Step 1: Minus 10 =
	    Step A: Minus 50 – Move the heaven bead up to touch the frame on the tens rod.
	    Step B: Adds 40 – Move all four earth beads up to touch the beam on the tens rod.
	
	Now we need to finish the formula by doing +2 on the ones rod, but we do not have enough earth beads to do +2 so, GET HELP from small friend formula and do +2.
	Step 2: Add 2 =
	    Step A: Add 5 – Move the heaven bead down to touch the beam on the ones rod.
	    Step B: Minus 3 – Move three earth beads down to touch the frame on the ones rod.
	
	(When we do −10 and +2, we get to keep 8 out of our game.)
	
	  − 10 +2 = − 8

SAI Speed Math Academy

EXAMPLE: 4

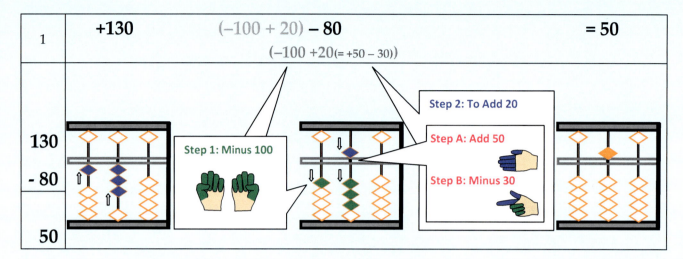

Problem	Action
+ 130	Set the numbers on their appropriate place value rods.

– 80	Now we need to –80 on the tens rod, but we do not have enough earth beads to do –80 on the tens rod. So, now we need to make use of the fact that **100 = 80 + 20**.
	When you want to –80 and you do not have enough beads:
	Use **–80 = –100 + 20** Big Friend formula to do your calculations.
	(This can be taught as using the same bead movement as for –8, but minus on the hundreds rod and add on the tens rod.)
	Step 1: Minus 100 – Move **one earth bead down** to touch the frame on the **hundreds rod.**
	Now we need to finish the formula by doing +20 on the tens rod, but we do not have enough earth bead to do +20 so, GET HELP from small friends formula and do +20.
	Step 2: Add 20 =
	  Step A: Add 50 – Move the heaven bead down to touch the beam on the tens rod.
	  Step B: Minus 30 – Move three earth beads down to touch the frame on the tens rod.
	There is nothing to do on the ones rod because the ones place number is zero
	(When we do –100 and +20, we get to keep 80 out of our game.)

ATTENTION

- Ask students to say the formula while they use it. This makes it easy for them to understand and follow through with all the steps in the formula.
- **Do not** say the small friend formula even when you are getting help from it. For instance, in example 4, JUST SAY "+20" while performing the small friend formula bead movements. Do not say the small friend formula out loud.

EXAMPLE: 5 $-80 = -100 + 20$

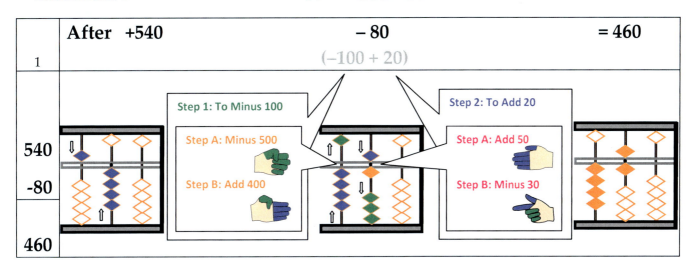

Problem	Action
+ 540	Set the numbers on their appropriate place value rods.

– 80	Now we need to –80 on the tens rod, but we do not have enough beads on the tens rod to do –80. So, now we need to make use of the fact that **100 = 80 + 20**.
	
	When you want to –80 and you do not have enough beads:
	Use $-80 = -100 + 20$ **Big Friend formula to do your calculations.**
	Now to do –100 you do not have enough beads so, GET HELP from small friend formula and do –100.
	Step 1: Minus 100 =
	  Step A: Minus 500 – Move the heaven bead up to touch the frame on the hundreds rod.
	  Step B: Add 400 – Move all four earth beads up to touch the beam on the hundreds rod.
	
	Now we need to finish the formula by doing +20 on the tens rod, but we do not have enough earth beads to do +20 so, GET HELP from small friend formula and do +20.
	Step 2: Add 20 =
	  Step A: Add 50 – Move the heaven bead down to touch the beam on the tens rod.
	  Step B: Minus 30 – Move three earth beads down to touch the frame on the tens rod.
	
	(When we do –100 and +20, we get to keep 80 out of our game.)
	
	$$-100 + 20 = -80$$
	
	There is nothing to do on the ones rod because the ones place number is zero.

SAMPLE PROBLEMS

$$-8 = -10 + 2 \qquad\qquad -80 = -100 + 20$$

TO INTRODUCE +2 OR +20 BY GETTING HELP FROM SMALL FRIENDS
FORMULA OF +2 = +5 –3 OR +20 = +50 –30

Work these problems a few times to study and understand the concept and the relationship between the beads moved.

1	2	3	4	5	6	7	8	9	10
43	24	64	55	52	210	134	174	144	143
22	- 08	- 08	- 21	- 18	- 80	- 80	- 80	- 80	- 18
- 11	- 08	- 18	- 18	- 08	- 80	- 18	- 88	- 08	- 88

TO INTRODUCE –10 OR –100 BY GETTING HELP FROM SMALL FRIENDS
FORMULA OF –10 = –50 +40 OR –100 = –500 +400

Work these problems a few times to study and understand the concept and the relationship between the beads moved.

1	2	3	4	5	6	7	8	9	10
54	63	54	71	62	610	234	532	534	644
- 10	- 08	- 08	- 18	- 18	- 180	- 80	- 188	- 80	- 180
02	- 08	- 18	- 18	- 08	- 80	- 88	- 98	- 18	- 18

1	2	3	4	5	6	7	8	9	10
29	84	93	86	77	47	55	31	267	284
25	30	61	- 22	26	57	- 18	42	397	250
- 18	- 08	- 18	- 18	- 88	- 98	- 19	- 28	- 198	- 88

POINTS TO REMEMBER

The rows above consist of sample problems to introduce this week's formula. Explain to your child when and how to use the formula. Work with the sample problems until your child understands the formula and that the formulas are to be used ONLY when there are not enough beads to add or subtract.

WEEK 5 – SPEED DICTATION

> Goal with speed dictation is to be able to increase the speed of child's calculating skill. Start with dictating 5 sets of numbers in 10 to 15 seconds and slowly increase giving more numbers in the same time.

1	2	3	4	5	6	7	8	9	10
04	06	07	08	09	04	01	05	08	02
01	03	01	- 03	- 05	04	05	03	01	02
02	- 07	- 02	02	01	- 06	01	- 07	- 05	03
- 04	02	- 01	02	- 02	02	- 03	04	01	- 04
03	01	- 01	- 07	03	01	02	- 01	- 02	05
10	40	30	60	80	50	60	10	20	70
20	40	10	10	- 50	30	- 20	10	30	- 40
10	- 30	- 20	- 20	20	10	- 10	- 20	- 10	10
40	- 30	50	- 20	- 10	- 30	30	50	50	10
- 70	20	- 40	- 10	20	- 20	30	- 30	- 80	- 20

5:S:4

1	2	3	4	5	6	7	8	9	10
10	30	40	50	80	20	70	60	20	30
40	50	10	- 20	- 10	70	- 30	10	10	50
10	- 70	40	30	- 40	- 80	- 10	- 20	20	- 20
- 20	40	- 70	- 10	20	40	20	- 20	10	- 10
- 10	40	40	40	10	- 10	- 10	30	- 40	- 40
05	06	01	02	04	05	07	05	02	06
03	03	05	03	01	03	02	01	04	01
- 06	- 07	- 02	- 01	01	01	- 05	02	03	- 07
04	06	01	04	- 03	- 07	01	- 03	- 06	05
- 06	- 08	04	01	04	04	- 05	- 01	02	- 01

5:S:5

SAI Speed Math Academy

WEEK 6 – SKILL BUILDING

WEEK 6 – SPEED DICTATION

Goal with speed dictation is to be able to increase the speed of child's calculating skill. Start with dictating 5 sets of numbers in 10 to 15 seconds and slowly increase giving more numbers in the same time.

1	2	3	4	5	6	7	8	9	10
03	02	04	03	06	01	06	08	05	07
05	05	01	02	01	05	01	- 02	- 01	- 05
01	- 04	01	01	- 03	- 01	01	- 03	02	03
60	50	60	10	30	40	20	20	70	80
10	10	10	40	20	10	60	50	10	10
- 40	20	- 20	30	10	- 30	- 50	- 30	- 40	- 70
- 20	- 60	- 20	- 20	30	20	20	10	30	40
- 06	03	01	- 01	01	- 02	- 07	04	- 03	01
01	01	02	- 01	- 04	05	04	01	02	- 04
01	- 05	- 09	- 04	02	- 07	- 05	- 07	- 04	05

6:S:1

1	2	3	4	5	6	7	8	9	10
50	20	30	70	40	10	80	60	90	30
10	40	20	- 30	50	20	- 40	20	- 80	40
20	10	- 10	10	- 60	10	20	- 70	70	10
06	02	04	05	03	05	06	08	09	02
01	04	02	- 02	05	01	- 02	- 05	- 04	05
- 04	- 03	02	01	- 06	- 02	03	02	- 02	01
01	02	- 08	01	03	03	- 02	03	03	- 03
- 10	20	10	20	10	10	- 10	80	- 40	- 60
20	- 40	20	10	10	40	- 10	- 60	20	50
- 70	- 10	- 30	- 70	- 40	- 90	40	20	10	- 60

6:S:2

WEEK 7 – LESSON 5 – INTRODUCING –7 CONCEPT

LESSON 5 – EXAMPLE

CONCEPTS OF THE WEEK

TO MINUS = MINUS 10, ADD BIG FRIEND $-7 = -10 + 3$ $-70 = -100 + 30$

EXAMPLE: 1

1	After	+ 20	- 07 (-10 +3)	= 13
20 - 07 13	ABACUS LOOKS LIKE	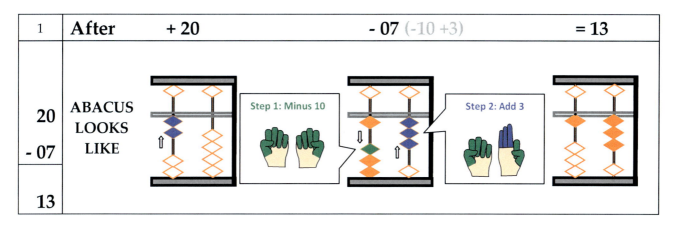		

Problem	Action
+ 20	Move **two earth beads** to touch the beam on the **tens rod.** There is nothing to do on the ones rod because ones place number is zero.
- 07	There is nothing to do on the tens rod because tens place number is zero. Now we need to –7 on the ones rod, but we do not have enough beads on the ones rod to do –7. So, now we need to make use of the fact that **10 = 7 + 3**. **When you want to –7 and you do not have enough beads:** Use $-7 = -10 + 3$ Big Friend formula to do your calculations. **Step 1: Minus 10** – Move **one earth bead down** to touch the frame on the **tens rod**. *(One earth bead on the tens rod is equal to '10')* *We know that there is a seven in the ten (7 + 3 = 10), so let us get help from 10 by sending it away from our game. However, we were supposed to –7, instead we did –10, which means we have sent 3 more than what we should have sent away. So, now we have to bring the 3 back into our game.* **Step 2: Add 3** – Move **three earth beads up** to touch the beam on the **ones rod**. *(When we do –10 and +3, we get to keep 7 out of our game.)* $-10 + 3 = -7$

EXAMPLE: 2   − 70 = − 100 + 30

1	+350	(−100 + 30) − 70	= 280
350 − 70 280		Step 1: Minus 100 Step 2: Add 30	

Problem	Action
+ 350	Set the numbers on their appropriate place value rods.
− 70	Now we need to −70 on the tens rod, but we do not have enough earth beads to do −70 on the tens rod. So, now we need to make use of the fact that **100 = 70 + 30**. **When you want to −70 and you do not have enough beads:** Use **−70 = −100 +30** **Big Friend formula to do your calculations.** *(This can be taught as using the same bead movement as for −7, however minus on the hundreds rod and add on the tens rod.)* <u>Step 1: Minus 100</u> – Move **one earth bead down** to touch the frame on the **hundreds rod**. <u>Step 2: Add 30</u> – Move **three earth beads up** to the beam on the **tens rod**. There is nothing to do on the ones rod because ones place number is zero.

ATTENTION

- Ask students to say the formula while they use it. This makes it easy for them to understand and follow through with all the steps in the formula. This will help with their presence of mind, and avoid confusion.
- Students are used to adding on the higher place value rod and subtracting on the working rod. Now, they may do −10 to follow this level's formula. However, instead of +3 they may do −3 (which is second half of the +9 formula) due to force of habit.
- When subtracting 17 (where they need to use the −7 formula) students will try −10 once and then +3. Make sure they understand that they have to −10 once for the ten in the 17 and **another** −10 to use the formula before finishing with **+3** while doing −7. E.g., 31 − 17
- When following the formula on the tens rod, students usually try −100 but then get confused and try to do +3 instead of +30. Make them understand that big friend of 70 is 30 and they help each other.

SAMPLE PROBLEMS

TO INTRODUCE –7 = –10 + 3 FORMULA

Work with these problems a few times to study and understand the concept and the relationship between the beads moved.

1	2	3	4	5	6	7	8	9	10
27	35	27	90	03	04	49	29	37	18
- 07	- 07	- 17	70	18	16	22	01	34	33
- 07	- 07	- 07	- 27	- 07	- 17	- 07	- 17	- 17	- 27

TO INTRODUCE –70 = – 100 + 30 FORMULA

Work with these problems a few times to study and understand the concept and the relationship between the beads moved.

1	2	3	4	5	6	7	8	9	10
70	60	99	48	69	180	150	268	445	500
30	50	11	52	41	20	- 70	- 77	- 187	- 170
- 70	- 77	- 77	- 77	- 77	- 70	- 17	- 77	- 179	- 17

1	2	3	4	5	6	7	8	9	10
95	94	72	95	99	74	75	375	166	563
- 17	73	49	55	05	81	95	- 87	145	- 179
- 34	- 19	- 17	- 17	83	- 37	- 87	- 78	- 87	- 79
11	- 17	- 71	- 88	- 77	- 78	- 79	- 170	41	- 177

POINTS TO REMEMBER

The rows above consist of sample problems to introduce this week's formula. Explain to your child when and how to use the formula. Work with the sample problems until your child understands the formula and that the formulas are to be used ONLY when there are not enough beads to add or subtract.

WEEK 7 – SPEED DICTATION

Goal with speed dictation is to be able to increase the speed of child's calculating skill. Start with dictating 5 sets of numbers in 10 to 15 seconds and slowly increase giving more numbers in the same time.

1	2	3	4	5	6	7	8	9	10
04	05	07	04	05	07	02	08	04	08
30	10	10	40	10	40	40	60	30	20
03	- 04	- 03	- 01	- 04	- 03	03	- 03	01	- 02
- 20	50	20	20	50	20	20	- 10	- 20	30
- 04	03	- 04	- 03	03	04	- 01	- 01	- 01	- 05
40	10	20	10	10	20	- 30	- 40	40	- 40
- 01	02	05	08	02	- 01	03	03	03	03
40	- 40	- 20	- 40	- 40	- 40	40	30	- 40	30
02	- 02	- 01	- 02	- 05	- 07	- 07	- 06	02	01
- 30	- 30	- 10	50	20	- 10	- 60	40	- 10	40

7:S:4

1	2	3	4	5	6	7	8	9	10
30	60	90	40	20	30	50	90	40	20
02	05	06	02	04	01	04	05	04	05
30	- 50	- 50	10	20	20	10	- 60	30	20
01	03	- 02	06	04	05	03	- 03	02	- 02
- 40	40	30	30	- 30	- 40	- 20	50	- 30	- 30
02	- 02	01	01	- 06	02	02	02	01	04
20	- 10	20	- 40	30	60	50	- 70	- 20	10
02	- 04	04	- 07	03	- 02	- 06	04	01	- 03
10	10	- 80	10	- 20	- 10	- 10	- 10	40	- 20
- 07	05	- 05	- 02	- 02	01	01	- 05	- 06	- 02

7:S:5

WEEK 8 – LESSON 6 – COMPLETING –7 USING SMALL FRIENDS FORMULA

CONCEPTS OF THE WEEK

TO MINUS = MINUS 10, ADD BIG FRIEND   – 7 = – 10 + 3   – 70 = – 100 + 30

– 7 = – 10 + 3
GET HELP FROM
–10 = –50 +40
+3 = +5 –2

– 70 = – 100 + 30
GET HELP FROM
–100 = –500 +400
+30 = +50 –20

By now, students should be at ease working with the –7 formula. In the previous lesson, all the problems where they had to use the formula were simple and students were able to follow the –7 formula directly. This week, they will learn to get help from our LEVEL–1 Small Friends formula of –10 and +3 in order to complete –7 formula. Students will understand this week's concept if you make them understand that they are "getting help" from LEVEL 1 formulas to do –7. You may choose to give a review quiz/dictation on lessons ten and thirteen in LEVEL 1 before introducing them to this week's lesson.

Example 1:   55 – 7 = 48
Set 55 on the abacus. Now to –7, we need to follow the formula of –7= –10 + 3, but we cannot do –10 directly. So to do –10, you have to follow –10 = –50 +40 formula from LEVEL – 1.

Example 2:   43 – 07 = 36
Set 43 on the abacus. Now to –7, we need to follow the formula of –7 = –10 +3. Here, you can directly do –10 however, you do not have enough ones bead on the ones rod to do +3. So to do +3, you get help from the +3 = +5 – 2 formula from LEVEL – 1.

Example 3:   52 – 07 = 45
Set 52 on the abacus. Here too we need to use the –7 = –10 +3 formula. However, both –10 and +3 cannot be done directly. To do both these steps, you have to get help from LEVEL – 1 Small Friends formulas for –10 = –50 +40 **and** +3 = +5 –2.

Example 4:   140 – 70 = 70
Set 140 on the abacus. To do –70, we now need to use the formula **–70** = **–100** +30. Here, to complete the steps you will have to get help from LEVEL – 1 Small Friends formulas for +30 = +50 –20.

SAI Speed Math Academy

LESSON 6 – EXAMPLE

EXAMPLE: 1

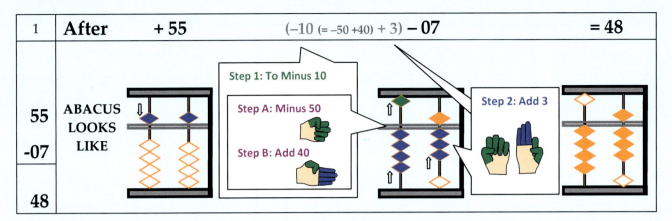

Problem	Action
+ 55	Set the numbers on their appropriate place value rods.

– 07	There is nothing to do on the tens rod because the tens place number is zero.
	
	Now we need to –7 on the ones rod, but we do not have enough beads on the ones rod to do –7. *(The heaven bead is in the game, but it does not have seven in it, so we cannot get help from it.)* So, now we need to make use of the fact that **10 = 7 + 3**.
	
	When you want to –7 and you do not have enough beads:
	Use **–7 = –10 + 3** Big Friend formula to do your calculations.
	Now to do –10 you do not have enough earth beads so, GET HELP from small friend formula and do –10.
	Step 1: Minus 10 =
	  Step A: Minus 50 – Move the heaven bead up to touch the frame on the tens rod.
	  Step B: Adds 40 – Move all four earth beads up to touch the beam on the tens rod.
	
	Now complete the –7 formula by doing +3 on the ones rod.
	 Step 2: Add 3 – Move **three earth beads up** to touch the beam on the **ones rod**.
	
	(When we do –10 and +3, we get to keep 7 out of our game.)
	
	$$-10 + 3 = -7$$

Pg 44   www.abacus-math.com

EXAMPLE: 2

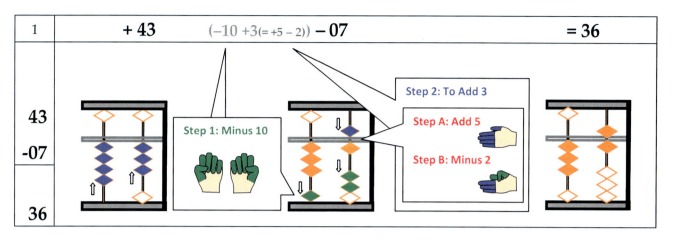

Problem	Action
+ 43	Set the numbers on their appropriate place value rods.

– 07	There is nothing to do on the tens rod because the tens place number is zero.
	
	Now we need to –7 on the ones rod, but we do not have enough beads on the ones rod to do –7. So, now we need to make use of the fact that **10 = 7 + 3**.
	
	When you want to –7 and you do not have enough beads:
	Use **–7 = –10 +3** Big Friend formula to do your calculations.
	Step 1: Minus 10 – Move **one earth bead down** to touch the frame on the **tens rod**.
	(One earth bead on the tens rod is equal to '10')
	
	Now we need to finish the formula by doing +3 on the ones rod, but we do not have earth beads to do +3 so, GET HELP from small friend formula and do +3.
	Step 2: Add 3 =
	  Step A: Add 5 – Move the heaven bead down to touch the beam on the ones rod.
	  Step B: Minus 2 – Move two earth beads down to touch the frame on the ones rod.
	
	(When we do –10 and +3, we get to keep 7 out of our game.)
	
	$$-10 + 3 = -7$$

EXAMPLE: 3

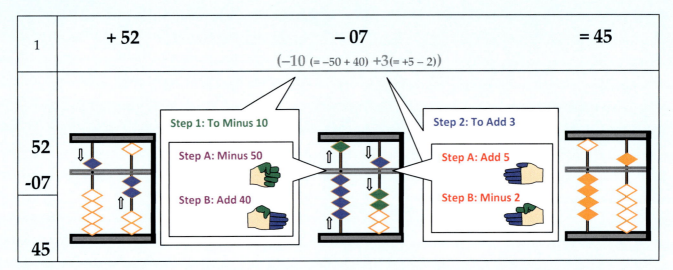

	+ 52	− 07 (−10 (= −50 + 40) +3(= +5 − 2))	= 45
1			
52			
-07			
45			

Problem	Action
+ 52	Set the numbers on their appropriate place value rods.

− 07	There is nothing to do on the tens rod because the tens place number is zero.
	
	Now we need to −7 on the ones rod, but we do not have enough beads on the ones rod to do −7. So, now we need to make use of the fact that **10 = 7 + 3.**
	
	When you want to −7 and you do not have enough beads:
	Use −7 = −10 +3 Big Friend formula to do your calculations.
	Now to do −10 you do not have enough beads so, GET HELP from small friend formula and do −10.
	Step 1: Minus 10 =
	   Step A: Minus 50 − Move the heaven bead up to touch the frame on the tens rod.
	   Step B: Adds 40 − Move all four earth beads up to touch the beam on the tens rod.
	
	Now we need to finish the formula by doing +3 on the ones rod, but we do not have enough earth beads to do +3 so, GET HELP from small friend formula and do +3.
	Step 2: Add 3 =
	   Step A: Add 5 − Move the heaven bead down to touch the beam on the ones rod.
	   Step B: Minus 2 − Move two earth beads down to touch the frame on the ones rod.
	
	(When we do −10 and +3, we get to keep 7 out of our game.)
	
	$$-10 + 3 = -7$$

EXAMPLE: 4

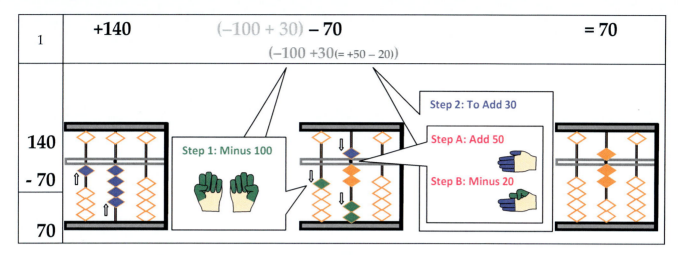

Problem	Action
+ 140	Set the numbers on their appropriate place value rods.
− 70	Now we need to −70 on the tens rod, but we do not have enough earth beads to do −70 on the tens rod. So, now we need to make use of the fact that **100 = 70 + 30**. **When you want to −70 and you do not have enough beads:** Use **−70 = −100 + 30** Big Friend formula to do your calculations. *(This can be taught as using the same bead movement as for −7, but minus on the hundreds rod and add on the tens rod.)* <u>Step 1: Minus 100</u> – Move **one earth bead down** to touch the frame on the **hundreds rod**. *Now we need to finish the formula by doing +30 on the tens rod, but we do not have enough earth bead to do +30 so, GET HELP from small friends formula and do +30.* <u>Step 2: Add 30</u> = <u>Step A: Add 50</u> – Move the heaven bead down to touch the beam on the tens rod. <u>Step B: Minus 20</u> – Move two earth beads down to touch the frame on the tens rod. There is nothing to do on the ones rod because the ones place number is zero *(When we do −100 and +30, we get to keep 70 out of our game.)*

ATTENTION

- It is highly likely that students get confused when they use small friends formula to do +3 in this lesson. Mostly they will confuse with +2 formula since they have been using it to do −8 for the past two weeks.
- Ask students to say the formula while they use it. This makes it easy for them to understand and follow through with all the steps in the formula.
- **Do not** say the small friend formula even when you are getting help from it. For instance, in example 4, JUST SAY "+30" while performing the small friend formula bead movements. Do not say the small friend formula out loud.

EXAMPLE: 5 $-70 = -100 + 30$

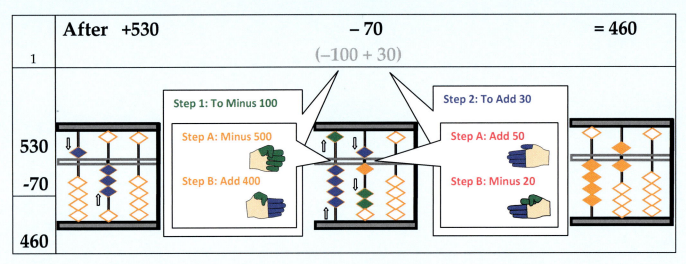

Problem	Action
+ 530	Set the numbers on their appropriate place value rods.

− 70	Now we need to −70 on the tens rod, but we do not have enough beads on the tens rod to do −70. So, now we need to make use of the fact that **100 = 70 + 30**.
	
	When you want to −70 and you do not have enough beads:
	Use −70 = −100 + 30 **Big Friend formula to do your calculations.**
	Now to do −100 you do not have enough beads so, GET HELP from small friend formula and do −100.
	Step 1: Minus 100 =
	    Step A: Minus 500 – Move the heaven bead up to touch the frame on the hundreds rod.
	    Step B: Add 400 – Move all four earth beads up to touch the beam on the hundreds rod.
	Now we need to finish the formula by doing +30 on the tens rod, but we do not have enough earth beads to do +30 so, GET HELP from small friend formula and do +30.
	Step 2: Add 30 =
	    Step A: Add 50 – Move the heaven bead down to touch the beam on the tens rod.
	    Step B: Minus 20 – Move two earth beads down to touch the frame on the tens rod.
	
	(When we do −100 and +30, we get to keep 70 out of our game.)
	
	    $-100 + 30 = -70$
	
	There is nothing to do on the ones rod because the ones place number is zero.

SAMPLE PROBLEMS

$$-7 = -10 + 3 \qquad\qquad -70 = -100 + 30$$

TO INTRODUCE +3 OR +30 BY GETTING HELP FROM SMALL FRIENDS
FORMULA OF +3 = +5 −2 OR +30 = +50 −20

Work these problems a few times to study and understand the concept and the relationship between the beads moved.

1	2	3	4	5	6	7	8	9	10
31	43	91	60	52	132	224	344	404	513
- 07	- 07	- 17	- 07	- 17	- 70	- 70	- 170	- 70	- 177
- 07	- 07	- 17	- 17	- 17	- 07	- 17	- 107	- 77	- 177

TO INTRODUCE −10 OR −100 BY GETTING HELP FROM SMALL FRIENDS
FORMULA OF −10 = −50 +40 OR −100 = −500 +400

Work these problems a few times to study and understand the concept and the relationship between the beads moved.

1	2	3	4	5	6	7	8	9	10
61	60	52	70	53	703	624	833	521	634
- 07	- 17	- 07	- 17	- 07	- 170	- 70	- 377	- 77	- 170
- 17	- 07	- 07	- 07	- 17	- 117	- 77	- 307	- 97	- 17

1	2	3	4	5	6	7	8	9	10
38	34	29	56	34	94	81	228	564	372
38	97	92	52	22	16	- 18	272	- 209	138
- 27	- 70	- 70	95	86	21	- 17	- 77	- 31	- 97
- 17	- 17	- 07	- 77	- 97	- 87	74	- 178	- 79	- 87

POINTS TO REMEMBER

The rows above consist of sample problems to introduce this week's formula. Explain to your child when and how to use the formula. Work with the sample problems until your child understands the formula and that the formulas are to be used ONLY when there are not enough beads to add or subtract.

WEEK 8 – SPEED DICTATION

> Goal with speed dictation is to be able to increase the speed of child's calculating skill. Start with dictating 5 sets of numbers in 10 to 15 seconds and slowly increase giving more numbers in the same time.

1	2	3	4	5	6	7	8	9	10
03	06	05	08	01	09	06	03	02	07
10	10	20	10	40	40	50	40	20	60
03	- 04	02	- 03	02	- 06	- 02	01	04	02
20	20	40	40	- 30	20	- 10	50	30	30
- 04	01	- 03	- 01	05	05	04	01	- 03	- 05
40	10	- 20	- 10	50	10	40	- 60	- 10	- 90
02	02	05	- 02	- 04	- 04	- 02	- 01	05	01
- 30	30	- 40	- 20	- 30	- 10	- 30	50	40	40
01	- 02	- 02	01	01	02	- 02	02	- 07	- 05
- 40	10	30	30	- 20	- 30	- 10	10	- 80	20

8:S:4

1	2	3	4	5	6	7	8	9	10
40	50	10	60	30	20	80	70	90	20
03	01	02	07	02	04	07	07	05	01
10	- 20	10	20	50	30	- 30	- 50	- 70	70
02	04	02	02	05	02	- 04	- 03	04	06
40	60	40	- 70	- 40	- 40	- 40	40	30	- 50
04	- 03	02	- 08	- 01	- 03	- 01	01	- 08	- 03
- 70	- 70	- 40	40	50	50	50	- 20	40	10
- 08	01	- 05	03	02	01	04	- 02	04	02
50	50	70	10	- 80	- 20	- 20	10	- 80	- 50
- 01	- 03	08	- 04	- 07	01	- 06	05	- 01	- 05

8:S:5

WEEK 9 – SKILL BUILDING

WEEK 9 – SPEED DICTATION

Goal with speed dictation is to be able to increase the speed of child's calculating skill. Start with dictating 5 sets of numbers in 10 to 15 seconds and slowly increase giving more numbers in the same time.

1	2	3	4	5	6	7	8	9	10
04	01	02	07	03	08	05	03	09	06
04	09	03	- 04	04	01	01	05	03	05
05	03	- 01	02	04	- 06	02	- 06	06	04
01	08	09	- 01	08	05	03	05	04	04
02	02	07	06	02	- 04	04	04	07	02
09	07	05	05	07	01	- 02	08	01	07
03	09	- 04	05	05	05	03	08	05	- 03
02	06	06	05	06	08	03	09	- 02	04
08	- 01	- 03	- 02	01	04	01	05	01	- 08
03	03	06	07	05	08	07	04	06	- 01

9:S:1

1	2	3	4	5	6	7	8	9	10
10	20	30	40	50	30	70	80	90	40
20	30	40	50	30	70	80	90	10	30
30	40	50	60	- 40	80	10	10	20	20
40	10	70	50	- 30	10	90	20	50	10
50	20	- 80	90	50	20	- 40	60	30	70
- 10	30	60	- 60	20	70	80	- 10	80	- 30
- 30	- 40	- 40	50	- 40	10	- 70	- 10	- 40	50
90	50	50	- 10	- 20	10	50	60	10	10
50	- 30	20	20	90	70	- 30	90	- 20	80
50	20	70	10	20	- 60	- 10	- 50	80	70

9:S:2

WEEK 10 – LESSON 7 – INTRODUCING –6 CONCEPT

LESSON 7 – EXAMPLE

CONCEPTS OF THE WEEK

TO MINUS = MINUS 10, ADD BIG FRIEND $-6 = -10 + 4$ $-60 = -100 + 40$

EXAMPLE: 1

1	After	+ 40	- 06 (-10 +4)	= 34
40 - 06 34	ABACUS LOOKS LIKE	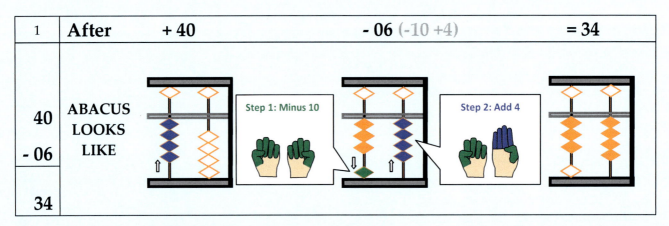		

Problem	Action
+ 40	Move **four earth beads** to touch the beam on the **tens rod**. There is nothing to do on the ones rod because ones place number is zero.
- 06	There is nothing to do on the tens rod because tens place number is zero. Now we need to **–6** on the ones rod, but we do not have enough beads on the ones rod to **–6**. So, now we need to make use of the fact that **10 = 6 + 4.** **When you want to –6 and you do not have enough beads:** **Use $-6 = -10 + 4$ Big Friend formula to do your calculations.** **Step 1: Minus 10** – Move **one earth bead down** to touch the frame on the **tens rod**. *(One earth bead on the tens rod is equal to '10')* *We know that there is a six in the ten (6 + 4 = 10), so let us get help from 10 by sending it away from our game. However, we were supposed to –6, instead we did –10, which means we have sent 4 more than what we should have sent away. So, now we have to bring the 4 back into our game.* **Step 2: Add 4** – Move **four earth beads up** to touch the beam on the **ones rod**. *(When we do –10 and +4, we get to keep 6 out of our game.)* $\boxed{-10 + 4 = -6}$

EXAMPLE: 2 $-60 = -100 + 40$

1	+200	(−100 + 40) − 60	= 140
200 - 60 140			

Problem	Action
+ 200	Set the numbers on their appropriate place value rods.
- 60	Now we need to –60 on the tens rod, but we do not have enough earth beads to do –60 on the tens rod. So, now we need to make use of the fact that **100 = 60 + 40.** **When you want to –60 and you do not have enough beads:** Use **–60 = –100 +40** **Big Friend formula to do your calculations.** *(This can be taught as using the same bead movement as for –6, however minus on the hundreds rod and add on the tens rod.)* <u>Step 1: Minus 100</u> – Move **one earth bead down** to touch the frame on the **hundreds rod**. <u>Step 2: Add 40</u> – Move **four earth beads up** to the beam on the **tens rod**. There is nothing to do on the ones rod because ones place number is zero.

ATTENTION
- Ask students to say the formula while they use it. This makes it easy for them to understand and follow through with all the steps in the formula. This will help with their presence of mind, and avoid confusion.
- Students are used to adding on the higher place value rod and subtracting on the working rod. Now, they may do –10 to follow this level's formula. However, instead of +4 they may do –4 (which is second half of the +9 formula) due to force of habit.
- When subtracting 16 (where they need to use the –6 formula) students will –10 once and then +4. Make sure they understand that they have to –10 once for the ten in the 16 and **another** –10 to use the formula before finishing with +4 while doing –6.   E.g., 25 – 16
- When following the formula on the tens rod, students usually –100 but then get confused and try to do +4 instead of +40. Make them understand that big friend of 60 is 40 and they help each other.

SAI Speed Math Academy

SAMPLE PROBLEMS

TO INTRODUCE –6 = –10 + 4 FORMULA

Work with these problems a few times to study and understand the concept and the relationship between the beads moved.

1	2	3	4	5	6	7	8	9	10
16	25	50	45	50	21	36	16	11	49
- 06	- 06	- 10	- 16	- 16	04	14	14	44	06
- 06	- 06	- 06	- 16	06	- 16	- 16	- 16	- 16	- 46

10:S:1

TO INTRODUCE –60 = –100 + 40 FORMULA

Work with these problems a few times to study and understand the concept and the relationship between the beads moved.

1	2	3	4	5	6	7	8	9	10
160	190	44	94	41	300	240	254	435	545
- 60	60	60	06	64	- 160	- 90	- 69	- 176	- 190
- 60	- 160	- 64	- 60	- 66	40	- 66	- 66	- 169	- 66

10:S:2

1	2	3	4	5	6	7	8	9	10
94	46	55	75	32	84	96	52	213	179
21	56	23	- 46	87	22	57	55	265	301
40	- 67	25	71	33	88	- 63	93	22	- 46
- 16	15	- 68	- 69	- 67	- 69	- 66	- 66	- 166	- 187

10:S:3

POINTS TO REMEMBER

The rows above consist of sample problems to introduce this week's formula. Explain to your child when and how to use the formula. Work with the sample problems until your child understands the formula and that the formulas are to be used ONLY when there are not enough beads to add or subtract.

WEEK 10 – SPEED DICTATION

Goal with speed dictation is to be able to increase the speed of child's calculating skill. Start with dictating 5 sets of numbers in 10 to 15 seconds and slowly increase giving more numbers in the same time.

1	2	3	4	5	6	7	8	9	10
01	09	03	04	05	07	08	06	02	08
05	07	05	01	06	04	01	03	03	- 07
09	06	03	05	04	05	02	05	08	08
09	03	04	06	07	03	05	05	03	- 06
- 04	- 01	- 02	07	04	01	- 02	- 07	07	05
05	- 02	04	- 03	- 02	08	01	05	05	09
08	05	- 03	06	- 02	- 02	- 04	- 06	- 07	02
- 02	- 04	06	- 02	03	- 04	06	08	05	07
05	07	09	09	- 01	07	- 03	06	08	08
07	09	01	02	05	01	08	06	- 01	- 04

10:S:4

1	2	3	4	5	6	7	8	9	10
50	60	30	20	70	40	80	10	70	90
80	- 40	30	50	- 40	20	- 30	40	50	10
20	50	20	- 60	20	40	- 20	90	70	90
50	- 30	30	40	- 10	30	10	10	10	60
60	10	60	30	50	30	10	80	90	90
- 30	90	- 70	50	30	50	40	20	20	20
20	- 30	80	60	50	50	10	70	70	- 30
70	70	60	10	60	70	50	30	30	40
50	20	10	70	- 20	20	20	60	50	- 70
30	50	70	70	80	60	50	40	- 40	80

10:S:5

WEEK 11 – LESSON 8 – COMPLETING –6 USING SMALL FRIENDS FORMULA

CONCEPTS OF THE WEEK
TO MINUS = MINUS 10, ADD BIG FRIEND – 6 = – 10 + 4   – 60 = – 100 + 40
– 6 = – 10 + 4   **GET HELP FROM**   –10 = –50 +40   +4 = +5 –1   – 60 = – 100 + 40   **GET HELP FROM**   –100 = –500 +400   +40 = +50 –10

By now, students should be at ease working with the –6 formula. In the previous lesson, all the problems where they had to use the formula were simple and students were able to follow the –6 formula directly. This week, they will learn to get help from our LEVEL–1 Small Friends formula of –10 and +4 in order to complete –6 formula. Students will understand this week's concept if you make them understand that they are "getting help" from LEVEL 1 formulas to do –6. You may choose to give a review quiz/dictation on lessons ten and fifteen in LEVEL 1 before introducing them to this week's lesson.

Example 1:   50 – 6 = 44
Set 50 on the abacus. Now to –6, we need to follow the formula of –6= –10 + 4, but we cannot do –10 directly. So to do –10, you have to follow –10 = –50 +40 formula from LEVEL – 1.

Example 2:   24 – 06 = 18
Set 24 on the abacus. Now to –6, we need to follow the formula of –6 = –10 +4. Here, you can directly do –10 however, you do not have enough ones bead on the ones rod to do +4. So to do +4, you get help from the +4 = +5 – 1 formula from LEVEL – 1.

Example 3:   51 – 06 = 45
Set 51 on the abacus. Here too we need to use the –6 = –10 +4 formula. However, both –10 and +4 cannot be done directly. To do both these steps, you have to get help from LEVEL – 1 Small Friends formulas for –10 = –50 +40 **and** +4 = +5 –1.

Example 4:   330 – 60 = 270
Set 330 on the abacus. To do –60, we now need to use the formula –60 = –100 +40. Here, to complete the steps you will have to get help from LEVEL – 1 Small Friends formulas for +40 = +50 –10.

LESSON 8 – EXAMPLE

EXAMPLE: 1

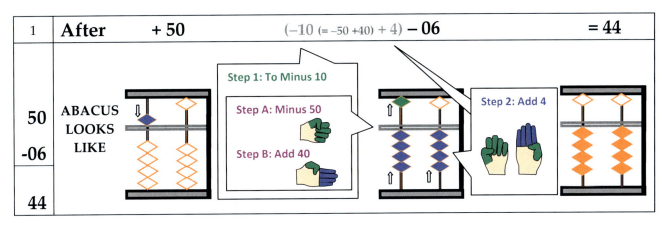

Problem	Action
+ 50	Set the numbers on their appropriate place value rods.

– 06	There is nothing to do on the tens rod because the tens place number is zero.
	
	Now we need to –6 on the ones rod, but we do not have enough beads on the ones rod to do –6. (*The heaven bead is in the game, but it does not have six in it, so we cannot get help from it.*) So, now we need to make use of the fact that **10 = 6 + 4.**
	
	When you want to –6 and you do not have enough beads:
	Use **–6 = –10 + 4** Big Friend formula to do your calculations.
	Now to do –10 you do not have enough earth beads so, GET HELP from small friend formula and do –10.
	Step 1: Minus 10 =
	   Step A: Minus 50 – Move the heaven bead up to touch the frame on the tens rod.
	   Step B: Adds 40 – Move all four earth beads up to touch the beam on the tens rod.
	
	Now complete the –6 formula by doing +4 on the ones rod.
	Step 2: Add 4 – Move **four earth beads up** to touch the beam on the **ones rod**.
	
	(When we do –10 and +4, we get to keep 6 out of our game.)
	
	$$-10 + 4 = -6$$

SAI Speed Math Academy

EXAMPLE: 2

| 1 | + 24 | (−10 +4(= +5 − 1)) − 06 | = 18 |

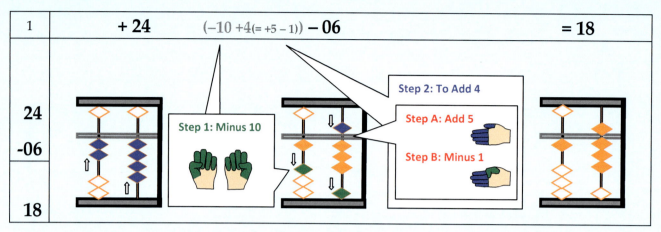

Problem	Action
+ 24	Set the numbers on their appropriate place value rods.
− 06	There is nothing to do on the tens rod because the tens place number is zero. Now we need to −6 on the ones rod, but we do not have enough beads on the ones rod to do −6. So, now we need to make use of the fact that **10 = 6 + 4**. **When you want to −6 and you do not have enough beads:** Use −6 = −10 +4 Big Friend formula to do your calculations. <u>Step 1: Minus 10</u> – Move **one earth bead down** to touch the frame on the **tens rod.** *(One earth bead on the tens rod is equal to '10')* *Now we need to finish the formula by doing +4 on the ones rod, but we do not have earth beads to do +4 so, GET HELP from small friend formula and do +4.* <u>Step 2: Add 4</u> = <u>Step A: Add 5</u> – Move the heaven bead down to touch the beam on the ones rod. <u>Step B: Minus 1</u> – Move one earth bead down to touch the frame on the ones rod. *(When we do −10 and +4, we get to keep 6 out of our game.)* $\boxed{-10 +4 = -6}$

EXAMPLE: 3

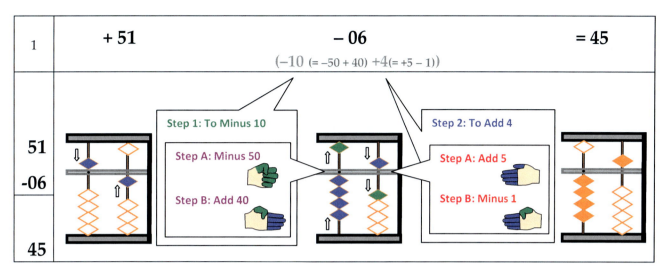

Problem	Action
+ 51	Set the numbers on their appropriate place value rods.
– 06	There is nothing to do on the tens rod because the tens place number is zero. Now we need to –6 on the ones rod, but we do not have enough beads on the ones rod to do –6. So, now we need to make use of the fact that **10 = 6 + 4.** **When you want to –6 and you do not have enough beads:** Use **–6 = –10 +4** **Big Friend formula to do your calculations.** *Now to do –10 you do not have enough beads so, GET HELP from small friend formula and do –10.* <u>Step 1: Minus 10 =</u> <u>Step A: Minus 50</u> – Move the heaven bead up to touch the frame on the tens rod. <u>Step B: Adds 40</u> – Move all four earth beads up to touch the beam on the tens rod. *Now we need to finish the formula by doing +4 on the ones rod, but we do not have enough earth beads to do +4 so, GET HELP from small friend formula and do +4.* <u>Step 2: Add 4 =</u> <u>Step A: Add 5</u> – Move the heaven bead down to touch the beam on the ones rod. <u>Step B: Minus 1</u> – Move one earth bead down to touch the frame on the ones rod. *(When we do –10 and +4, we get to keep 6 out of our game.)* $$-10 + 4 = -6$$

EXAMPLE: 4

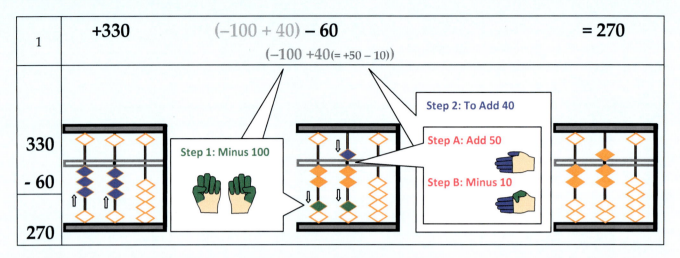

	+330	(–100 + 40) – 60	= 270
1		(–100 +40(= +50 – 10))	

Problem	Action
+ 330	Set the numbers on their appropriate place value rods.

– 60	Now we need to –60 on the tens rod, but we do not have enough earth beads to do –60 on the tens rod. So, now we need to make use of the fact that **100 = 60 + 40.**
	When you want to –60 and you do not have enough beads:
	Use **–60 = –100 + 40** **Big Friend formula to do your calculations.**
	(This can be taught as using the same bead movement as for –6, but minus on the hundreds rod and add on the tens rod.)
	Step 1: Minus 100 – Move **one earth bead down** to touch the frame on the **hundreds rod.**
	Now we need to finish the formula by doing +40 on the tens rod, but we do not have enough earth bead to do +40 so, GET HELP from small friends formula and do +40.
	Step 2: Add 40 =
	  Step A: Add 50 – Move the heaven bead down to touch the beam on the tens rod.
	  Step B: Minus 10 – Move one earth bead down to touch the frame on the tens rod.
	There is nothing to do on the ones rod because the ones place number is zero
	(When we do –100 and +40, we get to keep 60 out of our game.)

ATTENTION

- Ask students to say the formula while they use it. This makes it easy for them to understand and follow through with all the steps in the formula.
- **Do not** say the small friend formula even when you are getting help from it. For instance, in example 4, JUST SAY "+40" while performing the small friend formula bead movements. Do not say the small friend formula out loud.

EXAMPLE: 5 −60 = −100 + 40

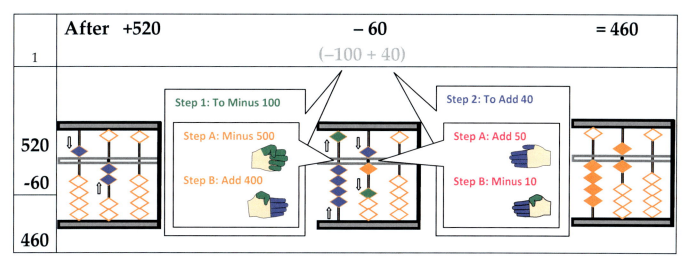

Problem	Action
+ 520	Set the numbers on their appropriate place value rods.

− 60	Now we need to −60 on the tens rod, but we do not have enough beads on the tens rod to do −60. So, now we need to make use of the fact that **100 = 60 + 40.**
	
	When you want to −60 and you do not have enough beads:
	Use −60 = −100 + 40 Big Friend formula to do your calculations.
	Now to do −100 you do not have enough beads so, GET HELP from small friend formula and do −100.
	Step 1: Minus 100 =
	    Step A: Minus 500 – Move the heaven bead up to touch the frame on the hundreds rod.
	    Step B: Add 400 – Move all four earth beads up to touch the beam on the hundreds rod.
	Now we need to finish the formula by doing +40 on the tens rod, but we do not have enough earth beads to do +40 so, GET HELP from small friend formula and do +40.
	Step 2: Add 40 =
	    Step A: Add 50 – Move the heaven bead down to touch the beam on the tens rod.
	    Step B: Minus 10 – Move one earth bead down to touch the frame on the tens rod.
	
	(When we do −100 and +40, we get to keep 60 out of our game.)
	
	$$-100 + 40 = -60$$
	
	There is nothing to do on the ones rod because the ones place number is zero.

SAMPLE PROBLEMS

$$-6 = -10 + 4 \qquad\qquad -60 = -100 + 40$$

TO INTRODUCE +4 OR +40 BY GETTING HELP FROM SMALL FRIENDS
FORMULA OF +4 = +5 –1 OR +40 = +50 –10

Work these problems a few times to study and understand the concept and the relationship between the beads moved.

1	2	3	4	5	6	7	8	9	10
55	42	24	50	93	61	221	234	312	713
- 13	- 06	- 06	- 16	- 60	- 06	- 60	- 160	- 60	- 460
44	- 06	- 16	- 16	- 16	- 16	- 46	- 16	- 16	- 116

TO INTRODUCE –10 OR –100 BY GETTING HELP FROM SMALL FRIENDS
FORMULA OF –10 = –50 +40 OR –100 = –500 +400

Work these problems a few times to study and understand the concept and the relationship between the beads moved.

1	2	3	4	5	6	7	8	9	10
74	50	61	60	81	601	265	511	713	812
- 16	- 06	- 16	- 06	- 16	- 60	249	- 66	- 466	- 260
- 16	- 06	- 14	- 06	- 16	- 66	- 166	- 196	- 86	- 66

1	2	3	4	5	6	7	8	9	10
73	89	93	45	37	81	34	65	255	378
53	35	45	- 16	55	- 66	45	74	189	32
28	- 66	43	54	- 26	54	- 26	53	203	- 166
- 16	42	- 66	- 69	- 26	- 36	- 06	- 46	- 366	- 96

POINTS TO REMEMBER

The rows above consist of sample problems to introduce this week's formula. Explain to your child when and how to use the formula. Work with the sample problems until your child understands the formula and that the formulas are to be used ONLY when there are not enough beads to add or subtract.

WEEK 11 – SPEED DICTATION

Goal with speed dictation is to be able to increase the speed of child's calculating skill. Start with dictating 5 sets of numbers in 10 to 15 seconds and slowly increase giving more numbers in the same time.

1	2	3	4	5	6	7	8	9	10
04	05	06	07	02	07	08	04	09	02
07	09	07	04	03	01	02	02	02	06
06	03	02	05	06	- 05	06	08	05	07
40	80	60	20	30	60	20	40	10	50
30	- 60	- 30	40	40	- 40	40	- 20	20	- 30
- 20	40	10	- 70	10	20	- 50	30	30	40
10	- 20	10	30	- 60	10	20	- 20	- 60	- 50
- 04	06	08	09	04	08	09	07	09	05
- 03	- 01	05	09	07	04	07	04	09	09
05	03	05	07	08	08	06	06	06	04

11:S:4

1	2	3	4	5	6	7	8	9	10
40	20	70	30	50	80	70	80	50	10
10	30	80	60	30	10	80	10	70	70
90	60	60	10	40	30	90	50	20	- 30
05	04	02	05	06	08	09	01	02	05
- 04	02	05	04	01	- 04	- 04	06	02	- 01
03	03	- 04	- 09	- 03	01	- 03	- 02	05	05
03	- 08	- 02	05	05	- 05	05	- 02	- 04	- 07
10	50	50	50	- 20	50	10	60	10	10
50	- 30	20	80	90	70	30	90	- 20	70
40	70	- 30	20	20	- 20	10	- 50	80	50

11:S:5

WEEK 12 – LESSON 9 – INTRODUCING –5 CONCEPT

LESSON 9 – EXAMPLE

CONCEPTS OF THE WEEK

TO MINUS = MINUS 10, ADD BIG FRIEND $- 5 = -10 + 5$ $-50 = -100 + 50$

EXAMPLE: 1

1	After	+ 30	- 05 (-10 +5)	= 25
30 - 05 25	ABACUS LOOKS LIKE	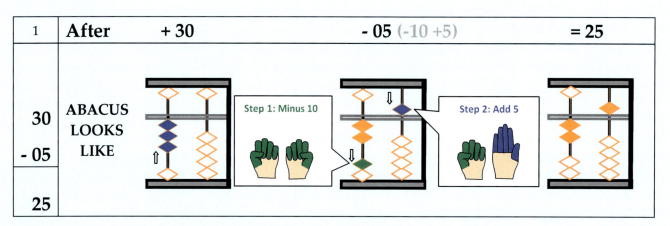		

Problem	Action
+ 30	Move **three earth beads** to touch the beam on the **tens rod.** There is nothing to do on the ones rod because ones place number is zero.
- 05	There is nothing to do on the tens rod because tens place number is zero. Now we need to –5 on the ones rod, but we do not have enough beads on the ones rod to –5. So, now we need to make use of the fact that **10 = 5 + 5**. **When you want to –5 and you do not have enough beads:** Use $-5 = -10 + 5$ **Big Friend formula to do your calculations.** **Step 1: Minus 10** – Move **one earth bead down** to touch the frame on the **tens rod.** *(One earth bead on the tens rod is equal to '10')* *We know that there is a five in the ten (5 + 5 = 10), so let us get help from 10 by sending it away from our game. However, we were supposed to –5, instead we did –10, which means we have sent 5 more than what we should have sent away. So, now we have to bring the 5 back into our game.* **Step 2: Add 5** – Move the **heaven bead down** to touch the beam on the **ones rod.** *(We bring the heaven bead to the game because we know that heaven bead is equal to five.)* ***(When we do –10 and +5, we get to keep 5 out of our game.)*** $\boxed{-10 + 5 = -5}$

EXAMPLE: 2 $-5 = -10 + 5$

| 1 | After | + 54 | - 05 $(-10(=-50+40)+5)$ | = 49 |

| 54 |
| - 05 |
| 49 |

Step 1: To Minus 10
Step A: Minus 50
Step B: Add 40
Step 2: Add 5

Problem	Action
+ 54	Set the numbers on their appropriate place value rods.

- 05	There is nothing to do on the tens rod because tens place number is zero.
	
	Now we need to **–5** on the ones rod, but we do not have enough beads on the ones rod to **–5**. So, now we need to make use of the fact that **10 = 5 + 5.**
	When you want to –5 and you do not have enough beads:
	Use $-5 = -10 + 5$ **Big Friend formula to do your calculations.**
	
	Now to do –10 you do not have enough earth beads so, GET HELP from small friend formula and do –10.
	Step 1: Minus 10 =
	   Step A: Minus 50 – Move the heaven bead up to touch the frame on the tens rod.
	   Step B: Adds 40 – Move all four earth beads up to touch the beam on the tens rod.
	
	Now, we need to complete the formula by doing +5 on the ones rod.
	Step 2: Add 5 – Move the **heaven bead down** to touch the beam on the **ones rod**.
	(We bring the heaven bead to the game because we know that heaven bead is equal to five.)
	
	(When we do –10 and +5, we get to keep 5 out of our game.)
	
	$-10 + 5 = -5$

SAI Speed Math Academy

EXAMPLE: 3   − 50 = − 100 + 50

1	+430	(-100 + 50) - 50	= 380
430 - 50 380		Step 1: Minus 100 Step 2: Add 50	

Problem	Action
+ 430	Set the numbers on their appropriate place value rods.
- 50	Now we need to –50 on the tens rod, but we do not have enough earth beads to do –50 on the tens rod. So, now we need to make use of the fact that **100 = 50 + 50**. **When you want to –50 and you do not have enough beads:** **Use –50 = –100 +50 Big Friend formula to do your calculations.** *(This can be taught as using the same bead movement as for –5, however minus on the hundreds rod and add on the tens rod.)* <u>Step 1: Minus 100</u> – Move **one earth bead down** to touch the frame on the **hundreds rod**. <u>Step 2: Add 50</u> – Move the **heaven bead down** to touch the beam on the **tens rod**. *(We bring the heaven bead to the game because we know that heaven bead is equal to fifty.)* There is nothing to do on the ones rod because ones place number is zero.

ATTENTION

- Ask students to say the formula while they use it. This makes it easy for them to understand and follow through with all the steps in the formula. This will help with their presence of mind, without which they will get confused.
- When subtracting 15 (where they need to use the –5 formula) students will –10 once and then +5. Make sure they understand that they have to –10 once for the ten in the 15 and **another** –10 to use the formula before finishing with **+5** while doing **–5**. E.g., 54 – 15
- When following the formula on the tens rod, students usually –100 but then get confused and try to do +5 instead of +50. Make them understand that big friend of 50 is 50 and they help each other.

EXAMPLE: 4   − 50 = − 100 + 50   − 5 = − 10 + 5

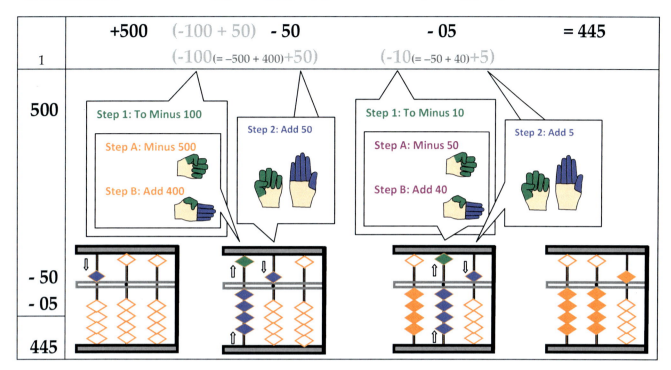

Problem	Action
+ 500	Set the numbers on their appropriate place value rods.

− 50	**When you want to −50 and you do not have enough beads:**
	Use −50 = −100 +50 Big Friend formula to do your calculations.
	Step 1: Minus 100 =
	    Step A: Minus 500 – Move the heaven bead up to touch the frame on the hundreds rod.
	    Step B: Add 400 – Move all four earth beads up to touch the beam on the hundreds rod.
	Now finish the formula by doing +50 on the tens rod.
	There is nothing to do on the ones rod because ones place number is zero.

− 05	**To do −5 there is not enough beads:**
	Use −5 = −10 +5 Big Friend formula to do your calculations.
	Step 1: Minus 10 =
	    Step A: Minus 50 – Move the heaven bead up to touch the frame on the tens rod.
	    Step B: Adds 40 – Move all four earth beads up to touch the beam on the tens rod.
	Now finish the formula by doing +5 on the ones rod.

ATTENTION

Example: 500 − 55 = 445 (500 − 50 − 05 = 445)

Please make sure that your student understands that they have to get help from −100 or −10 Small Friends formula and then finish by doing +50 or + 5 depending on which rod they are subtracting from. Some students get confused with this concept in this lesson.

SAMPLE PROBLEMS

TO INTRODUCE –5 = –10 + 5 and –50 = –100 + 50 FORMULA

Work with these problems a few times to study and understand the concept and the relationship between the beads moved.

1	2	3	4	5	6	7	8	9	10
27	41	55	48	64	125	135	205	101	249
- 05	- 05	- 15	05	- 50	- 50	- 55	- 55	- 51	- 55
- 05	- 15	- 05	- 15	- 05	- 15	- 55	- 15	- 15	- 55

TO INTRODUCE –10 OR –100 BY GETTING HELP FROM SMALL FRIENDS FORMULA OF –10 = –50 + 40 OR –100 = –500 + 400

Work with these problems a few times to study and understand the concept and the relationship between the beads moved.

1	2	3	4	5	6	7	8	9	10
51	62	53	99	65	201	216	329	511	625
- 15	- 15	- 05	05	- 15	- 150	- 55	- 155	- 150	- 155
- 15	- 25	- 35	- 55	- 05	- 05	- 55	- 155	- 15	- 125

1	2	3	4	5	6	7	8	9	10
49	84	46	67	47	23	89	87	129	237
84	55	17	55	61	54	75	55	193	145
26	12	83	43	53	67	24	- 26	- 150	- 150
- 17	- 50	96	- 55	- 78	- 55	- 85	38	- 25	- 97
- 55	- 75	- 55	- 55	- 55	11	- 55	- 05	- 98	- 55

POINTS TO REMEMBER

The rows above consist of sample problems to introduce this week's formula. Explain to your child when and how to use the formula. Work with the sample problems until your child understands the formula and that the formulas are to be used ONLY when there are not enough beads to add or subtract.

WEEK 12 – SPEED DICTATION

Goal with speed dictation is to be able to increase the speed of child's calculating skill. Start with dictating 5 sets of numbers in 10 to 15 seconds and slowly increase giving more numbers in the same time.

1	2	3	4	5	6	7	8	9	10
03	08	05	06	09	01	07	02	03	05
02	05	09	07	01	06	- 04	07	05	06
07	03	07	05	09	07	05	07	01	05
50	60	20	50	50	30	50	80	40	20
- 10	- 30	20	20	30	50	- 10	- 20	10	- 30
40	10	- 40	10	- 60	- 80	40	- 20	- 30	50
- 30	- 20	20	- 70	10	30	- 50	- 10	50	- 10
02	09	07	04	02	02	04	09	06	05
02	06	02	05	05	06	03	05	04	07
08	07	09	05	08	08	08	04	01	04

12:S:4

1	2	3	4	5	6	7	8	9	10
60	30	40	70	90	80	10	20	40	30
50	60	20	10	- 60	- 30	40	60	20	20
40	40	30	20	40	- 30	90	10	40	50
05	09	06	04	08	05	04	09	08	05
02	- 04	- 05	- 02	- 04	01	01	- 06	01	02
01	- 01	03	05	02	- 03	- 02	02	- 07	- 04
- 04	- 04	03	- 03	01	04	04	04	03	02
50	50	- 70	90	20	60	20	50	90	80
20	40	50	20	70	30	50	50	30	- 40
30	10	60	50	50	90	- 10	- 60	80	10

12:S:5

SAI Speed Math Academy   Pg 69

WEEK 13 – LESSON 10 – INTRODUCING –4 CONCEPT

LESSON 10 – EXAMPLE

CONCEPTS OF THE WEEK
TO MINUS = MINUS 10, ADD BIG FRIEND $-4 = -10 + 6$ $-40 = -100 + 60$

EXAMPLE: 1

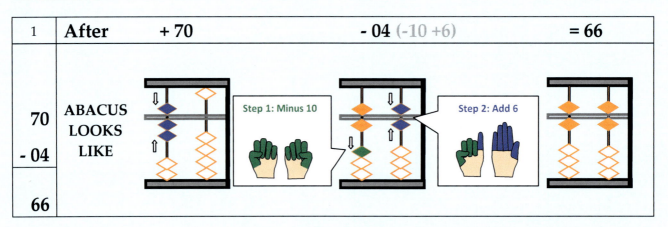

Problem	Action
+ 70	Set the number on the appropriate place value rod.
– 04	There is nothing to do on the tens rod because tens place number is zero. Now we need to –4 on the ones rod, but we do not have enough beads on the ones rod to –4. So, now we need to make use of the fact that **10 = 4 + 6**. **When you want to –4 and you do not have enough beads:** Use $-4 = -10 + 6$ **Big Friend formula to do your calculations.** **Step 1: Minus 10** – Move **one earth bead down** to touch the frame on the **tens rod**. *(One earth bead on the tens rod is equal to '10')* We know that there is a four in the ten (4 + 6 = 10), so let us get help from 10 by sending it away from our game. However, we were supposed to –4, instead we did –10, which means we have sent 6 more than what we should have sent away. So, now we have to bring the 6 back into our game. **Step 2: Add 6** – Move the **heaven bead and one earth bead** to touch the beam on the **ones rod**. *(When we do –10 and +6, we get to keep 4 out of our game.)* $\qquad\qquad\qquad\qquad\qquad\qquad\qquad\qquad\qquad$ $\boxed{-10 + 6 = -4}$

EXAMPLE: 2 $\qquad -4 = -10 + 6$

1	After	+ 51	- 04	= 47

$(-10_{(= -50 + 40)} + 6)$

Step 1: To Minus 10
Step A: Minus 50
Step B: Add 40
Step 2: Add 6

51
- 04
47

Problem	Action
+ 51	Set the numbers on their appropriate place value rods.
- 04	There is nothing to do on the tens rod because tens place number is zero. Now we need to –4 on the ones rod, but we do not have enough beads on the ones rod to –4. So, now we need to make use of the fact that **10 = 4 + 6.** **When you want to –4 and you do not have enough beads:** **Use –4 = – 10 + 6 Big Friend formula to do your calculations.** *Now to do –10 you do not have enough earth beads so, GET HELP from small friend formula and do –10.* <u>Step 1: Minus 10</u> = <u>Step A: Minus 50</u> – Move the heaven bead up to touch the frame on the tens rod. <u>Step B: Adds 40</u> – Move all four earth beads up to touch the beam on the tens rod. *Now, we need to complete the formula by doing +6 on the ones rod.* <u>Step 2: Add 6</u> – Move the **heaven bead and one earth bead** to touch the beam on the **ones rod**. *(When we do –10 and +6, we get to keep 4 out of our game.)* $\boxed{-10 + 6 = -4}$

ATTENTION
Ask students to say the formula while they use it. This makes it easy for them to understand and follow through with all the steps. This will also ensure that they use the correct formula. Some of them will confuse with small friend formula and big friend formula by doing –10 and then +1 instead of doing + 6.

EXAMPLE: 3   − 40 = − 100 + 60

1	+330	(-100 + 60) - 40		= 290
330 - 60 290		Step 1: Minus 100	Step 2: Add 60	

Problem	Action
+ 330	Set the numbers on their appropriate place value rods.
- 40	Now we need to –40 on the tens rod, but we do not have enough earth beads to do –40 on the tens rod. So, now we need to make use of the fact that **100 = 40 + 60**. **When you want to –40 and you do not have enough beads:** Use **–40 = –100 +60** Big Friend formula to do your calculations. *(This can be taught as using the same bead movement as for* **–4**, *however minus on the hundreds rod and add on the tens rod.)* Step 1: Minus 100 – Move **one earth bead down** to touch the frame on the **hundreds rod**. Step 2: Add 60 – Move the **heaven bead and one earth bead down** to touch the beam on the **tens rod**. There is nothing to do on the ones rod because ones place number is zero.

ATTENTION

From this week we will learn to subtract 4, 3, 2, and 1 using Big Friends formula.
Please make sure that children understand that 4, 3, 2, and 1 have small friend formula and big friend formula.

- When the heaven bead is in the game then they have to use small friend formula (–4 = –5 + 1) to finish calculating.
- When the heaven bead is not in the game AND there are not enough earth beads to –4 then they have to use Big Friend formula (–4 = –10 + 6).
- When subtracting 14 (where they need to use the –4 formula) students will –10 once and then **+6**. Make sure they understand that they have to –10 once for the ten in the 14 and **another** –10 to use the formula before finishing with **+6** while doing **–4**. E.g., 20 – 14
- When following the formula on the tens rod, students usually –100 but then get confused and try to do +6 instead of +60. Make them understand that big friend of 40 is 60 and they help each other.

SAMPLE PROBLEMS

TO INTRODUCE −4 = −10 + 6 and −40 = −100 + 60 FORMULA

Work with these problems a few times to study and understand the concept and the relationship between the beads moved.

1	2	3	4	5	6	7	8	9	10
25	30	52	66	50	350	148	230	320	601
- 04	- 04	- 14	- 14	- 14	- 140	- 44	- 74	- 140	- 444
- 04	- 14	- 04	- 14	- 24	- 144	- 44	- 44	- 44	- 14

TO INTRODUCE −10 OR −100 BY GETTING HELP FROM SMALL FRIENDS
FORMULA OF −10 = −50 + 40 OR −100 = −500 + 400

Work with these problems a few times to study and understand the concept and the relationship between the beads moved.

1	2	3	4	5	6	7	8	9	10
74	61	65	99	95	135	605	516	700	500
- 14	- 14	- 14	01	- 44	- 44	- 144	- 44	- 450	- 140
- 14	- 14	- 04	- 54	- 04	- 44	- 114	- 24	- 104	- 14

1	2	3	4	5	6	7	8	9	10
75	78	45	94	24	85	75	78	255	189
52	26	65	11	27	37	- 41	33	86	204
63	- 51	- 04	- 46	53	64	74	60	- 94	36
- 54	- 14	- 49	38	- 44	- 49	- 47	- 94	- 146	- 144
- 57	- 24	- 18	- 53	- 17	- 46	- 34	- 56	- 78	- 241

POINTS TO REMEMBER

The rows above consist of sample problems to introduce this week's formula. Explain to your child when and how to use the formula. Work with the sample problems until your child understands the formula and that the formulas are to be used ONLY when there are not enough beads to add or subtract.

SAI Speed Math Academy

WEEK 13 – SPEED DICTATION

Goal with speed dictation is to be able to increase the speed of child's calculating skill. Start with dictating 5 sets of numbers in 10 to 15 seconds and slowly increase giving more numbers in the same time.

1	2	3	4	5	6	7	8	9	10
05	04	03	02	08	09	07	06	01	08
60	70	60	90	20	50	40	50	80	30
04	07	05	06	07	01	- 06	02	09	07
50	- 40	20	40	60	40	60	- 40	40	80
- 06	05	02	- 05	- 02	03	09	02	07	05
40	30	- 60	50	30	70	50	90	20	60
08	01	05	01	01	02	04	06	- 03	09
40	10	70	50	80	- 40	30	70	- 10	10
07	03	- 01	08	06	- 03	01	05	05	- 07
80	30	10	- 10	40	70	30	80	60	90

13:S:4

1	2	3	4	5	6	7	8	9	10
40	20	90	30	50	30	70	40	80	60
09	03	08	06	03	07	08	02	03	04
10	60	60	10	- 40	80	10	40	- 20	90
- 07	04	02	05	- 03	01	09	03	01	07
- 30	20	50	30	50	20	- 40	30	10	20
05	03	04	09	02	07	08	05	07	02
80	80	- 10	50	- 40	10	40	50	90	80
04	05	05	05	- 02	01	05	07	05	03
90	- 30	30	80	90	50	70	80	30	90
09	05	- 03	02	02	- 06	09	03	05	04

13:S:5

WEEK 14 – LESSON 11 – INTRODUCING –3 CONCEPT

LESSON 11 – EXAMPLE

CONCEPTS OF THE WEEK

TO MINUS = MINUS 10, ADD BIG FRIEND $-3 = -10 + 7$ $-30 = -100 + 70$

EXAMPLE: 1

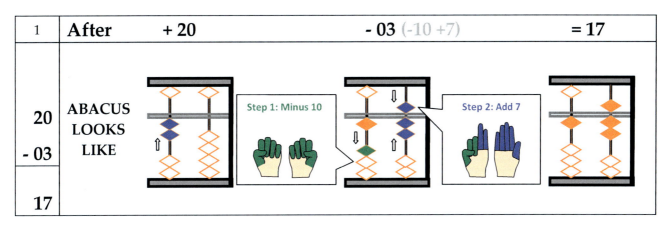

| 1 | After | + 20 | - 03 (-10 +7) | = 17 |

| 20 |
| - 03 |
| 17 |
| ABACUS LOOKS LIKE |

Problem	Action
+ 20	Move **two earth beads** to touch the beam on the **tens rod.** There is nothing to do on the ones rod because ones place number is zero.
- 03	There is nothing to do on the tens rod because tens place number is zero. Now we need to –3 on the ones rod, but we do not have enough beads on the ones rod to –3. So, now we need to make use of the fact that **10 = 3 + 7.** **When you want to –3 and you do not have enough beads:** Use $-3 = -10 + 7$ Big Friend formula to do your calculations. Step 1: Minus 10 – Move **one earth bead down** to touch the frame on the **tens rod**. *(One earth bead on the tens rod is equal to '10')* *We know that there is a three in the ten (3 + 7 = 10), so let us get help from 10 by sending it away from our game. However, we were supposed to –3, instead we did –10, which means we have sent 7 more than what we should have sent away. So, now we have to bring the 7 back into our game.* Step 2: Add 7 – Move the **heaven bead down** and **two earth beads** to touch the beam on the **ones rod**. *(When we do –10 and +7, we get to keep 3 out of our game.)* $\boxed{-10 + 7 = -3}$

SAI Speed Math Academy

EXAMPLE: 2   − 3 = − 10 + 7

1	After	+ 51	- 03 (-10(= −50 + 40)+7)	= 48
51 - 03 48			**Step 1: To Minus 10** Step A: Minus 50 Step B: Add 40	**Step 2: Add 7**

Problem	Action
+ 51	Set the numbers on their appropriate place value rods.

- 03	There is nothing to do on the tens rod because tens place number is zero.
	
	Now we need to –3 on the ones rod, but we do not have enough beads on the ones rod to –3. So, now we need to make use of the fact that **10 = 3 + 7**.
	When you want to –3 and you do not have enough beads:
	Use **–3 = – 10 + 7** Big Friend formula to do your calculations.
	
	Now to do –10 you do not have enough earth beads so, GET HELP from small friend formula and do –10.
	Step 1: Minus 10 =
	   Step A: Minus 50 – Move the heaven bead up to touch the frame on the tens rod.
	   Step B: Adds 40 – Move all four earth beads up to touch the beam on the tens rod.
	
	Now, we need to complete the formula by doing +7 on the ones rod.
	Step 2: Add 7 – Move the **heaven bead down** and **two earth beads** to touch the beam on the **ones rod**.
	
	(When we do –10 and +7, we get to keep 3 out of our game.)
	
	$\boxed{-10 + 7 = -3}$

EXAMPLE: 3 −30 = −100 + 70

1	+500	(−100(= −500 + 400)+ 70) − 30	= 470
500 − 30 470			

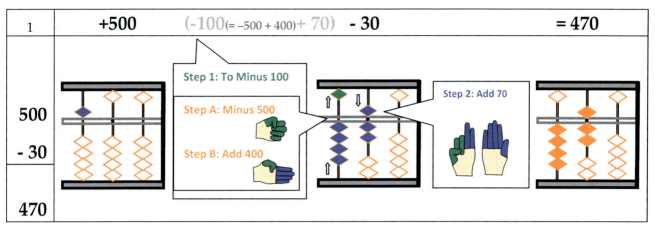

Problem	Action
+ 500	Set the numbers on their appropriate place value rods.

− 30	Now we need to −30 on the tens rod, but we do not have enough earth beads to do −30 on the tens rod. So, now we need to make use of the fact that **100 = 30 + 70**.
	When you want to −30 and you do not have enough beads:
	Use **−30 = −100 +70** **Big Friend formula to do your calculations.**
	(This can be taught as using the same bead movement as for −3, however minus on the hundreds rod and add on the tens rod.)
	
	Step 1: Minus 100 =
	  Step A: Minus 500 – Move the heaven bead up to touch the frame on the hundreds rod.
	  Step B: Add 400 – Move all four earth beads up to touch the beam on the hundreds rod.
	Step 2: Add 70 – Move the **heaven bead down** and **two earth beads** to touch the beam on the **tens rod**.
	
	There is nothing to do on the ones rod because ones place number is zero.

ATTENTION

- Ask students to say the formula while they use it. This makes it easy for them to understand and follow through with all the steps in the formula. This will help with their presence of mind, and avoid confusion.
- When subtracting 13 (where they need to use the −3 formula) students will −10 once and then +7. Make sure they understand that they have to −10 once for the ten in the 13 and **another** −10 to use the formula before finishing with +7 while doing −3. E.g., 50 − 13
- When following the formula on the tens rod, students usually −100 but then get confused and try to do +7 instead of +70. Make them understand that big friend of 30 is 70 and they help each other.

SAMPLE PROBLEMS

TO INTRODUCE –3 = –10 + 7 and –30 = –100 + 70 FORMULA

Work with these problems a few times to study and understand the concept and the relationship between the beads moved.

1	2	3	4	5	6	7	8	9	10
35	64	55	51	75	147	100	303	222	500
- 03	- 33	- 13	- 13	- 33	- 33	- 33	- 83	- 63	- 130
- 03	- 03	- 13	33	- 33	- 33	- 13	- 13	43	- 33

TO INTRODUCE –10 OR –100 BY GETTING HELP FROM SMALL FRIENDS FORMULA OF –10 = –50 + 40 OR –100 = –500 + 400

Work with these problems a few times to study and understand the concept and the relationship between the beads moved.

1	2	3	4	5	6	7	8	9	10
80	73	50	69	60	204	135	500	650	553
- 33	- 13	- 10	33	- 13	- 43	- 33	- 330	- 133	- 33
- 13	- 13	- 13	- 53	53	- 13	- 33	- 33	- 33	- 73

1	2	3	4	5	6	7	8	9	10
46	55	97	89	39	81	56	65	265	185
48	- 19	95	25	41	45	55	74	89	95
18	78	- 38	- 33	68	- 93	- 34	- 35	26	- 68
- 33	- 34	- 35	25	- 34	49	63	- 44	- 133	- 33
- 69	- 33	- 38	- 73	- 35	- 53	- 57	- 13	- 33	27

POINTS TO REMEMBER

The rows above consist of sample problems to introduce this week's formula. Explain to your child when and how to use the formula. Work with the sample problems until your child understands the formula and that the formulas are to be used ONLY when there are not enough beads to add or subtract.

WEEK 14 – SPEED DICTATION

Goal with speed dictation is to be able to increase the speed of child's calculating skill. Start with dictating 5 sets of numbers in 10 to 15 seconds and slowly increase giving more numbers in the same time.

1	2	3	4	5	6	7	8	9	10
14	59	33	25	76	95	83	65	39	46
07	02	07	10	- 40	04	40	02	10	70
21	55	66	55	74	21	25	45	11	19
- 40	- 04	05	10	08	30	- 04	- 02	09	60
27	35	44	77	13	44	65	39	41	12
01	90	- 01	03	06	10	- 08	50	09	- 04
28	- 25	16	22	88	39	39	12	- 16	16
- 10	80	30	80	05	60	08	- 10	80	- 09
51	11	24	33	27	19	41	21	22	89
60	02	90	- 02	05	- 20	- 80	08	- 03	80

1	2	3	4	5	6	7	8	9	10
26	72	45	62	21	32	43	69	59	98
90	40	04	09	05	05	06	50	05	80
83	59	63	54	63	61	66	11	33	- 18
50	06	90	30	70	40	50	08	40	09
49	- 34	29	- 22	21	29	- 41	22	51	55
- 95	70	07	90	06	- 03	90	90	20	- 04
62	45	55	76	29	- 44	32	44	33	57
30	02	- 60	- 04	50	05	40	30	60	- 30
14	21	77	13	- 42	12	92	41	95	13
41	20	05	20	07	03	- 60	- 02	50	40

WEEK 15 – LESSON 12 – INTRODUCING –2 CONCEPT

LESSON 12 – EXAMPLE

CONCEPTS OF THE WEEK

TO MINUS = MINUS 10, ADD BIG FRIEND   – 2 = – 10 + 8   – 20 = – 100 + 80

EXAMPLE: 1

1	After	+ 10	– 02 (-10 +8)	= 08
10 - 02 08	ABACUS LOOKS LIKE		Step 1: Minus 10 Step 2: Add 8	

Problem	Action
+ 10	Move **one earth bead** to touch the beam on the **tens rod.** There is nothing to do on the ones rod because ones place number is zero.
– 02	There is nothing to do on the tens rod because tens place number is zero. Now we need to **–2** on the ones rod, but we do not have enough beads on the ones rod to –2. So, now we need to make use of the fact that **10 = 2 + 8.** **When you want to –2 and you do not have enough beads:** Use **–2 = – 10 + 8** Big Friend formula to do your calculations. **Step 1: Minus 10** – Move **one earth bead down** to touch the frame on the **tens rod.** *(One earth bead on the tens rod is equal to '10')* *We know that there is a two in the ten (2 + 8 = 10), so let us get help from 10 by sending it away from our game. However, we were supposed to –2, instead we did –10, which means we have sent 8 more than what we should have sent away. So, now we have to bring the 8 back into our game.* **Step 2: Add 8** – Move the **heaven bead down** and **three earth beads** to touch the beam on the **ones rod**. *(When we do –10 and +8, we get to keep 2 out of our game.)* $$-10 + 8 = -2$$

EXAMPLE: 2 − 2 = − 10 + 8

1	After	+ 50	- 02	= 48
			(-10(= −50 + 40)+8)	
50 - 02 48		Step 1: To Minus 10 Step A: Minus 50 Step B: Add 40	Step 2: Add 8	

Problem	Action
+ 50	Set the numbers on their appropriate place value rods.
- 02	There is nothing to do on the tens rod because tens place number is zero. Now we need to –2 on the ones rod, but we do not have enough beads on the ones rod to –2. So, now we need to make use of the fact that **10 = 2 + 8.** **When you want to –2 and you do not have enough beads:** Use −2 = − 10 + 8 **Big Friend formula to do your calculations.** *Now to do –10 you do not have enough earth beads so, GET HELP from small friend formula and do –10.* <u>Step 1: Minus 10</u> = <u>Step A: Minus 50</u> – Move the heaven bead up to touch the frame on the tens rod. <u>Step B: Adds 40</u> – Move all four earth beads up to touch the beam on the tens rod. *Now, we need to complete the formula by doing +8 on the ones rod.* <u>Step 2: Add 8</u> – Move the **heaven bead down** and **three earth beads** to touch the beam on the **ones rod**. *(When we do –10 and +8, we get to keep 2 out of our game.)* $$-10 + 8 = -2$$

SAI Speed Math Academy

EXAMPLE: 3   −20 = −100 + 80

1	+510	(−100 (= −500 + 400) + 80) −20		= 490
510 − 20 490				

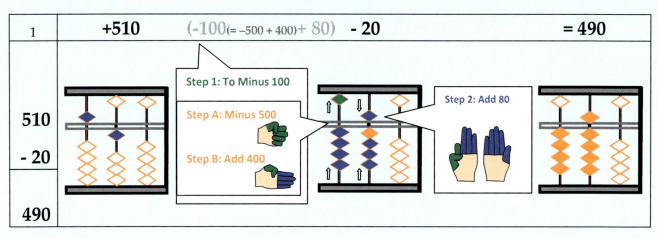

Problem	Action
+ 510	Set the numbers on their appropriate place value rods.

− 20	Now we need to −20 on the tens rod, but we do not have enough earth beads to do −20 on the tens rod. So, now we need to make use of the fact that **100 = 20 + 80**.
	When you want to −20 and you do not have enough beads:
	Use **−20 = −100 + 80** **Big Friend formula to do your calculations.**
	(This can be taught as using the same bead movement as for −2, however minus on the hundreds rod and add on the tens rod.)
	Step 1: Minus 100 =
	   Step A: Minus 500 – Move the heaven bead up to touch the frame on the hundreds rod.
	   Step B: Add 400 – Move all four earth beads up to touch the beam on the hundreds rod.
	   Step 2: Add 80 – Move the **heaven bead down** and **three earth beads** to touch the beam on the **tens rod**.
	There is nothing to do on the ones rod because ones place number is zero.

ATTENTION

- Ask students to say the formula while they use it. This makes it easy for them to understand and follow through with all the steps in the formula. This will help with their presence of mind and avoid confusion.
- When subtracting 12 (where they need to use the −2 formula) students will −10 once and then +8. Make sure they understand that they have to −10 once for the ten in the 12 and **another** −10 to use the formula before finishing with **+8** while doing **−2**. E.g., 40 − 12
- When following the formula on the tens rod, students usually −100 but then get confused and try to do +8 instead of +80. Make them understand that big friend of 20 is 80 and they help each other.

SAMPLE PROBLEMS

TO INTRODUCE –2 = –10 + 8 and –20 = –100 + 80 FORMULA

Work with these problems a few times to study and understand the concept and the relationship between the beads moved.

1	2	3	4	5	6	7	8	9	10
43	82	53	51	60	132	110	212	130	533
- 02	- 12	- 12	- 12	- 22	- 22	- 22	- 62	- 22	- 22
- 02	- 12	- 12	20	- 22	- 22	12	- 12	- 22	- 122

TO INTRODUCE –10 OR –100 BY GETTING HELP FROM SMALL FRIENDS
FORMULA OF –10 = –50 + 40 OR –100 = –500 + 400

Work with these problems a few times to study and understand the concept and the relationship between the beads moved.

1	2	3	4	5	6	7	8	9	10
72	72	60	99	50	122	123	510	600	509
- 22	- 12	- 12	02	- 02	- 72	- 62	- 220	- 120	- 20
- 12	- 12	02	- 52	52	- 22	- 12	- 22	- 232	12

1	2	3	4	5	6	7	8	9	10
75	64	69	49	79	94	55	149	152	184
52	57	89	71	84	15	67	152	75	38
- 46	47	- 36	37	- 46	- 29	- 42	- 32	- 36	109
- 62	- 18	- 62	- 48	- 21	- 33	- 32	262	- 42	- 122
- 17	- 12	- 12	- 25	- 42	68	54	- 82	- 75	- 125

POINTS TO REMEMBER

The rows above consist of sample problems to introduce this week's formula. Explain to your child when and how to use the formula. Work with the sample problems until your child understands the formula and that the formulas are to be used ONLY when there are not enough beads to add or subtract.

WEEK 15 – SPEED DICTATION

Goal with speed dictation is to be able to increase the speed of child's calculating skill. Start with dictating 5 sets of numbers in 10 to 15 seconds and slowly increase giving more numbers in the same time.

1	2	3	4	5	6	7	8	9	10
95	84	73	62	48	59	77	26	51	38
60	70	80	90	20	50	40	50	08	30
44	41	55	16	27	21	- 16	42	25	17
50	- 03	20	30	- 60	40	58	- 01	40	80
- 16	28	- 24	- 45	- 12	33	09	93	57	95
40	50	60	50	70	90	15	09	20	06
88	21	15	91	11	22	04	26	93	59
- 40	05	- 07	10	80	- 01	30	70	10	- 01
17	43	- 11	38	56	- 13	13	65	95	17
02	01	40	90	40	09	50	20	40	09

15:S:4

1	2	3	4	5	6	7	8	9	10
26	29	99	39	52	39	77	48	86	69
40	03	10	06	03	07	08	02	03	04
- 35	61	81	14	- 41	84	51	44	- 27	95
08	04	02	05	03	01	09	03	01	07
11	24	56	33	25	29	- 44	33	15	- 34
40	03	04	20	02	07	08	05	07	02
79	85	- 12	54	43	12	47	52	91	18
03	05	05	30	- 02	01	05	- 07	05	- 20
58	34	35	88	95	59	42	82	37	65
70	- 05	- 70	- 07	20	- 06	09	03	05	04

15:S:5

WEEK 16 – LESSON 13 – INTRODUCING –1 CONCEPT

LESSON 13 – EXAMPLE

CONCEPTS OF THE WEEK

TO MINUS = MINUS 10, ADD BIG FRIEND $-1 = -10 + 9$ $-10 = -100 + 90$

EXAMPLE: 1

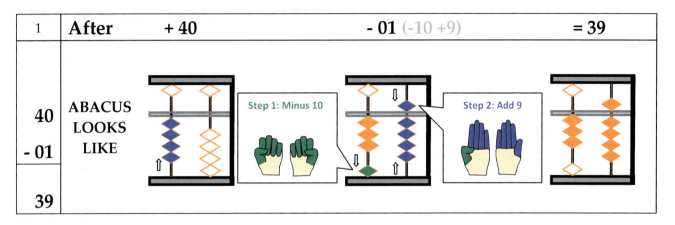

1	After	+ 40	- 01 (-10 +9)	= 39
40 - 01 39	ABACUS LOOKS LIKE			

Problem	Action
+ 40	Move **four earth beads** to touch the beam on the **tens rod**. There is nothing to do on the ones rod because ones place number is zero.
- 01	There is nothing to do on the tens rod because tens place number is zero. Now we need to **–1** on the ones rod, but we do not have enough beads on the ones rod to –1. So, now we need to make use of the fact that **10 = 1 + 9.** **When you want to –1 and you do not have enough beads:** Use $-1 = -10 + 9$ Big Friend formula to do your calculations. <u>Step 1: Minus 10</u> – Move **one earth bead down** to touch the frame on the **tens rod**. *(One earth bead on the tens rod is equal to '10')* *We know that there is a one in the ten (1 + 9 = 10), so let us get help from 10 by sending it away from our game. However, we were supposed to –1, instead we did –10, which means we have sent 9 more than what we should have sent away. So, now we have to bring the 9 back into our game.* <u>Step 2: Add 9</u> – Move the **heaven bead down** and **four earth beads** to touch the beam on the **ones rod**. *(When we do –10 and +9, we get to keep 1 out of our game.)* $$-10 + 9 = -1$$

SAI Speed Math Academy

EXAMPLE: 2   −1 = −10 + 9

1	After	+ 50	- 01 (-10(= −50 + 40)+9)	= 49
50 - 01 49			Step 1: To Minus 10 Step A: Minus 50 Step B: Add 40 Step 2: Add 9	

Problem	Action
+ 50	Set the numbers on their appropriate place value rods.

- 01	There is nothing to do on the tens rod because tens place number is zero.
	
	Now we need to –1 on the ones rod, but we do not have enough beads on the ones rod to –1. So, now we need to make use of the fact that **10 = 1 + 9**.
	When you want to –1 and you do not have enough beads:
	Use **–1 = – 10 + 9** Big Friend formula to do your calculations.
	
	Now to do –10 you do not have enough earth beads so, GET HELP from small friend formula and do –10.
	Step 1: Minus 10 =
	   Step A: Minus 50 – Move the heaven bead up to touch the frame on the tens rod.
	   Step B: Adds 40 – Move all four earth beads up to touch the beam on the tens rod.
	
	Now, we need to complete the formula by doing +9 on the ones rod.
	Step 2: Add 9 – Move the **heaven bead down** and **four earth beads** to touch the beam on the **ones rod**.
	
	(When we do –10 and +9, we get to keep 1 out of our game.)
	
	− 10 + 9 = − 1

EXAMPLE: 3   − 10 = − 100 + 90

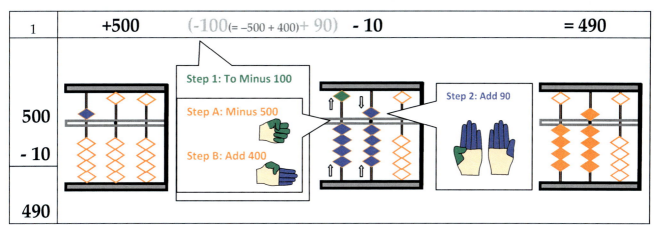

Problem	Action
+ 500	Set the numbers on their appropriate place value rods.
- 10	Now we need to –10 on the tens rod, but we do not have enough earth beads to do –10 on the tens rod. So, now we need to make use of the fact that **100 = 10 + 90**. **When you want to –10 and you do not have enough beads:** Use **–10 = –100 + 90** Big Friend formula to do your calculations. *(This can be taught as using the same bead movement as for –1, however minus on the hundreds rod and add on the tens rod.)* <u>Step 1: Minus 100</u> = <u>Step A: Minus 500</u> – Move the heaven bead up to touch the frame on the hundreds rod. <u>Step B: Add 400</u> – Move all four earth beads up to touch the beam on the hundreds rod. <u>Step 2: Add 90</u> – Move the **heaven bead down** and **four earth beads** to touch the beam on the **tens rod**. There is nothing to do on the ones rod because ones place number is zero.

ATTENTION

- Ask students to say the formula while they use it. This makes it easy for them to understand and follow through with all the steps in the formula. This will help with their presence of mind and avoid confusion.
- When subtracting 11 (where they need to use the –1 formula) students will –10 once and then +9. Make sure they understand that they have to –10 once for the ten in the 11 and **another** –10 to use the formula before finishing with **+9** while doing **–1**. E.g., 30 – 11
- When following the formula on the tens rod, students usually –100 but then get confused and try to do +9 instead of +90. Make them understand that big friend of 10 is 90 and they help each other.

SAI Speed Math Academy

SAMPLE PROBLEMS

TO INTRODUCE –1 = –10 + 9 and –10 = –100 + 90 FORMULA

Work with these problems a few times to study and understand the concept and the relationship between the beads moved.

1	2	3	4	5	6	7	8	9	10
65	50	21	61	40	88	120	210	115	500
- 11	- 10	- 11	- 11	10	12	- 11	- 01	- 11	- 110
- 11	- 01	- 01	- 11	- 41	- 11	- 11	- 110	- 11	- 111

TO INTRODUCE –10 OR –100 BY GETTING HELP FROM SMALL FRIENDS
FORMULA OF –10 = –50 + 40 OR –100 = –500 + 400

Work with these problems a few times to study and understand the concept and the relationship between the beads moved.

1	2	3	4	5	6	7	8	9	10
50	71	60	99	50	300	121	600	731	500
- 01	- 11	- 11	01	- 11	- 10	- 71	- 110	- 181	- 10
10	- 11	51	- 51	61	- 41	- 01	- 41	- 111	- 41

1	2	3	4	5	6	7	8	9	10
79	43	89	94	87	68	55	49	52	193
31	34	11	17	82	27	76	52	75	37
- 60	- 17	- 51	- 38	61	65	24	- 11	- 36	270
- 11	- 11	11	- 23	- 21	- 11	- 11	- 41	- 48	- 191
61	15	- 41	- 11	- 11	51	- 98	- 49	11	- 16

POINTS TO REMEMBER

The rows above consist of sample problems to introduce this week's formula. Explain to your child when and how to use the formula. Work with the sample problems until your child understands the formula and that the formulas are to be used ONLY when there are not enough beads to add or subtract.

WEEK 16 – SPEED DICTATION

Goal with speed dictation is to be able to increase the speed of child's calculating skill. Start with dictating 5 sets of numbers in 10 to 15 seconds and slowly increase giving more numbers in the same time.

1	2	3	4	5	6	7	8	9	10
56	29	65	37	48	41	73	99	67	81
29	23	80	41	52	14	42	02	- 43	59
30	75	17	55	99	60	56	95	51	16
19	16	66	22	60	37	71	17	26	- 45
24	55	24	- 14	45	93	- 42	82	32	39
- 16	- 73	85	33	91	- 21	99	- 41	15	74
53	88	17	37	- 72	53	01	72	- 48	- 13
61	45	53	- 11	- 11	- 44	69	- 23	96	48
89	- 17	91	56	- 12	12	- 26	95	22	46
07	44	- 88	99	33	16	67	13	35	48

16:S:4

1	2	3	4	5	6	7	8	9	10
55	55	36	65	26	14	26	99	44	67
69	15	45	22	16	57	45	- 67	55	38
- 21	26	38	87	44	35	54	57	- 33	65
97	36	65	55	- 33	78	89	13	59	56
49	49	- 34	29	71	- 21	11	98	68	74
11	88	43	- 46	69	64	- 23	59	39	44
46	- 42	55	23	15	59	45	- 16	87	17
11	59	16	25	19	- 65	63	59	55	28
- 14	76	78	79	45	44	09	44	- 22	- 42
46	34	- 32	- 32	- 52	39	- 14	- 25	54	55

16:S:5

WEEK 17 – LESSON 14 – BORROWING OR REGROUPING FROM HUNDREDS ROD TO SUBTRACT ON ONES ROD

CONCEPTS OF THE WEEK – BORROWING FROM THE HUNDRED'S ROD

TO MINUS = MINUS 10, ADD BIG FRIEND

TO MINUS 10 = If you do not have enough beads to –10 in a formula

USE = –10 = –100 + 90   and/or –100 = –500 + 400

– 9 = –10 + 1	– 4 = –10 + 6
– 8 = –10 + 2	– 3 = –10 + 7
– 7 = –10 + 3	– 2 = –10 + 8
– 6 = –10 + 4	– 1 = –10 + 9
– 5 = –10 + 5	– 10 = –100 + 90

What do you need to succeed?

Passion, patience, practice, tenacity and commitment.

LESSON 14 – EXAMPLE

EXAMPLE 1:   100 – 01 = 99   (–1= –10 + 9)

In the example it is not possible to do –10 because the tens rod has no beads in the game. So, we have to substitute **–10 = –100 + 90** and finish with the rest of the formula by doing **+9** on the ones rod.

To do **–01 = –10** (**–100 + 90**) **+ 9**

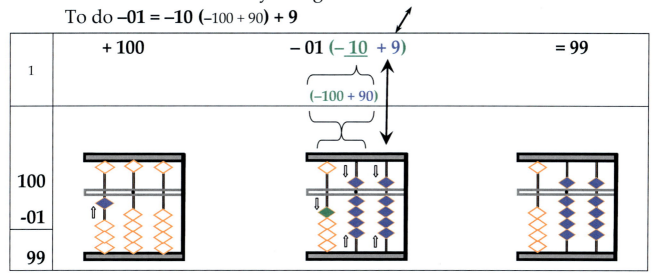

Problem	Action
+ 100	Set the numbers on their appropriate place value rods.
– 01	There is nothing to do on the tens rod because tens place number is zero. Now we need to –1 on the ones rod, however we do not have enough beads on the ones rod to –1. So, now we need to use the big friend formula of –1 = –10 + 9 *Here, beads on the tens place rod are not in the game, so we cannot do –10 directly. Now to do –10, you need to GET HELP from BIG FRIEND FORMULA of –10 and complete the step.* *Big friend formula for –10 = –100 + 90* *We have to substitute –10 in the –1= –10 + 9 with –10 = –100 + 90* *Now, –1 = –10 (–100 + 90) + 9* <u>Step 1: Minus 10</u> – **Move one earth bead down to touch the frame on the hundreds rod** *(One earth bead on the hundreds rod is equal to '100')* **and do + 90 by moving the heaven bead and all earth beads to touch the beam on the tens rod.** *Now, we need to complete the formula by doing +9 on the ones rod.* <u>Step 2: Add 9</u> – **Move the heaven bead and the four earth beads to touch the beam on the ones rod.** *(Be sure to make students understand that + 9 has to be done on the ones rod because we are trying to –1 on the ones rod.)*

SAI Speed Math Academy

EXAMPLE 2:   103 – 07 = 97   (–7 = –10 + 3)

To do – 07 = –10 (–100 + 90) + 3 (+5 –2)

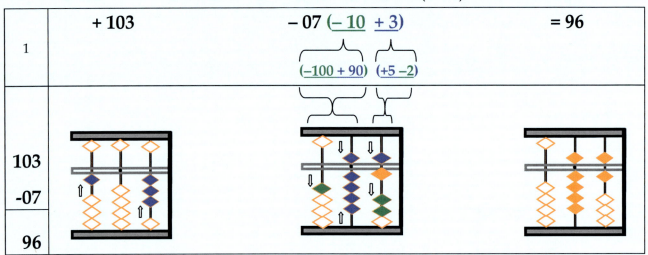

Problem	Action
+ 103	Set the numbers on their appropriate place value rods.
- 07	There is nothing to do on the tens rod because tens place number is zero. Now we need to –7 on the ones rod, however we do not have enough beads on the ones rod to do –7. So, now we need to use the big friend formula of –7 = –10 +3. *Here, beads on the tens place rod are not in the game, so we cannot do –10 directly. Now to do –10, you need to GET HELP from BIG FRIEND FORMULA of –10 and complete the step.* *Big friend formula for –10 = –100 + 90* We have to substitute –10 in the –7 = –10 + 3 with –10 = –100 + 90 Now, –7 = –10 (–100 + 90) + 3 Step 1: Minus 10 – **Move one earth bead down to touch the frame on the hundreds rod** (One earth bead on the hundreds rod is equal to '100') **and do + 90 by moving the heaven bead and all earth beads to touch the beam on the tens rod.** *Now, we need to complete the formula by doing +3 on the ones rod.* Step 2: Add 3 = GET HELP from SMALL FRIENDS FORMULA OF + 3. **Move the heaven bead down to touch the beam on the ones rod and move two earth beads down to touch the frame on the ones rod.** *(Be sure to make students understand that + 3 has to be done on the ones rod because we are trying to –7 on the ones rod.)*

EXAMPLES 3: 500 – 05 = 495   (–5 = –10 + 5)

Formula for –5 = –10 + 5

At times you may not have enough beads to use the –10 = –100 + 90 formula.

In such a case you may have to use –10 = –100 (–500 + 400) + 90

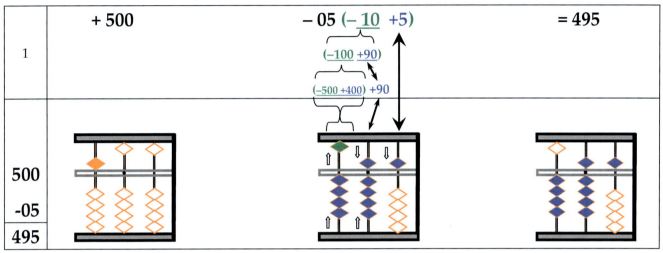

Problem	
+ 500	Set the numbers on their appropriate place value rods.
- 05	There is nothing to do on the tens rod because tens place number is zero. Now we need to –5 on the ones rod, however we do not have enough beads on the ones rod to –5. So, now we need to use the big friend formula of –5 = –10 +5. *Here, beads on the tens place rod are not in the game, so we cannot do –10 directly. Now to do –10, you need to GET HELP from BIG FRIEND FORMULA of –10 and complete the step.* *Big friend formula for –10 = –100 + 90* However, *here there are not enough earth beads to –100. Now, GET HELP from small friend formula of –100 = –500 +400.* **Now, –5 = –10 (–100 (–500 + 400) + 90) + 5** <u>Step 1: Minus 10</u> – **Move the heaven bead up to touch the frame and four earth beads up to touch the beam on the hundreds rod to do –100 AND move all the beads to touch the beam on the tens rod to complete + 90.** <u>Step 2: Add 5</u> – Move the **heaven bead down to touch the beam on the ones rod.** *(Be sure to make students understand that +5 (which is the second half of the –5 formula) has to be done on the ones rod because we are trying to –5 on the ones rod.)*

EXAMPLES 4: 503 − 08 = 495   (−8 = −10 + 2)

In this example you will not be able to −8 directly. In such situations get help from appropriate small and big friend formulas to finish the original formula of −8.

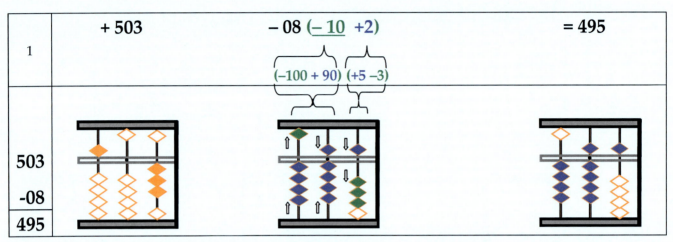

Problem	
+ 503	Set the numbers on their appropriate place value rods.
- 08	There is nothing to do on the tens rod because tens place number is zero. Now we need to −8 on the ones rod, however we do not have enough beads on the ones rod to −8. So, now we need to use the big friend formula of −8 = −10 + 2. *Here, beads on the tens place rod are not in the game, so we cannot do −10 directly.* *Now to do −10, you GET HELP from BIG FRIEND FORMULA of +10 and complete the step.* *Big friend formula for −10 = −100 +90* However, *here there are not enough earth beads to −100. Now, GET HELP from small friend formula of −100 = −500 +400.* Now, −8 = −10 (−100 (−500 + 400) + 90) + 2. <u>Step 1: Minus 10</u> – **Move the heaven bead up to touch the frame and four earth beads up to touch the beam on the hundreds rod to do −100 AND move all the beads to touch the beam on the tens rod to complete + 90.** <u>Step 2: Add 2</u> – **GET HELP from SMALL FRIENDS FORMULA OF + 2.** **Move the heaven bead down to touch the beam on the ones rod and move three earth beads down to touch the frame on the ones rod.** *(Be sure to make students understand that +2 has to be done on the ones rod because we are trying to −8 on the ones rod.)*

ATTENTION

This week's concept may be challenging to younger children. With tenacity and patience, they will master this concept.

The following may help the younger students and those who are having a hard time understanding the concept:

- Ask them to hold a finger on the frame under the rod (working rod) where they need to minus a number and try to solve the problem. This will help them to keep track of where they need to add or subtract.

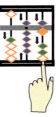

- Ask students to say the formula while they use it. This makes it easy for them to understand and follow through with all the steps. This will also ensure that they use the correct formula.

- In situations where they **get help** from small or big friends formulas, students should not be saying those formulas.

If the above idea does not help, you can ask them to place their finger under the rod they need to minus and 'minus one' on any higher place value rod wherever possible and move all the beads to touch the beam on all rods in between that rod and their working rod. Then they must finish with the rest of the formula on the rod above their finger. This is a short cut for students to understand this week's concept. *Please use this method of explaining at your own discretion.*

One common mistake almost all students make is double subtracting.

Children are used to doing –10 on the tens place rod all through this level. However, from this lesson they learn to substitute –10 with –100 + 90 in certain situations.

In such case, due to habit, even though they do –100 and + 90 to do –10, children will absent mindedly go back and minus another ten on the tens rod.

E.g., **104 – 5 = –10** (–100 + 90) **+ 5 = 99**

Students will do the above steps as per this week's concept, however due to force of habit they will go back and minus another ten on the tens rod and arrive at 89 as their answer.

Ask them to say the formula as they move the required beads to keep themselves on track and avoid making this mistake. With patience and practice this mistake can be overcome successfully.

LESSON 14 – SAMPLE PROBLEMS

$$-1 = -10 + 9 \qquad\qquad -10 = -100 + 90$$

Work these problems a few times to study and understand the concept and the relationship between the beads moved.

For Example 1:

1	2	3	4	5	6	7	8	9	10
100 - 01	100 - 02	100 - 03	100 - 04	100 - 05	100 - 06	100 - 07	100 - 08	100 - 09	140 - 46

For Example 2:

1	2	3	4	5	6	7	8	9	10
104 - 09	104 - 08	103 - 08	104 - 07	103 - 07	102 - 07	104 - 06	103 - 06	102 - 06	101 - 06

For Example 3:

1	2	3	4	5	6	7	8	9	10
500 - 01	700 - 202	800 - 303	540 - 44	551 - 55	560 - 66	530 - 37	520 - 28	598 - 99	512 - 14

For Example 4:

1	2	3	4	5	6	7	8	9	10
504 - 09	604 - 108	513 - 18	674 - 177	733 - 237	562 - 67	504 - 06	823 - 326	532 - 36	941 - 446

POINTS TO REMEMBER

The rows above consist of sample problems to introduce this week's formula. Explain to your child when and how to use the formula. Work with the sample problems until your child understands the formula and that the formulas are to be used ONLY when there are not enough beads to add or subtract.

LESSON 14 – PRACTICE PROBLEMS

We have given a few problems in the rows below where students have had the most difficulty.

1	*2*	*3*	*4*	*5*	*6*	*7*	*8*	*9*	*10*
101 - 11	100 - 11	100 - 01	110 - 11	102 - 12	100 - 12	100 - 02	110 - 12	103 - 13	100 - 13

1	*2*	*3*	*4*	*5*	*6*	*7*	*8*	*9*	*10*
100 - 03	110 - 13	104 - 14	100 - 14	100 - 04	110 - 14	105 - 15	100 - 15	100 - 05	110 - 15

1	*2*	*3*	*4*	*5*	*6*	*7*	*8*	*9*	*10*
106 - 16	100 - 16	100 - 06	110 - 16	107 - 17	100 - 17	100 - 07	110 - 17	108 - 18	100 - 18

1	*2*	*3*	*4*	*5*	*6*	*7*	*8*	*9*	*10*
100 - 08	110 - 18	109 - 19	100 - 19	100 - 09	110 - 19	124 - 19	104 - 19	104 - 09	114 - 19

1	*2*	*3*	*4*	*5*	*6*	*7*	*8*	*9*	*10*
514 - 19	124 - 18	103 - 18	104 - 08	113 - 18	724 - 228	123 - 17	104 - 17	102 - 07	114 - 17

1	*2*	*3*	*4*	*5*	*6*	*7*	*8*	*9*	*10*
633 - 137	123 - 16	104 - 16	102 - 06	111 - 16	101 - 06	510 - 11	521 - 22	532 - 33	543 - 44

WEEK 17 – SPEED DICTATION

Goal with speed dictation is to be able to increase the speed of child's calculating skill. Start with dictating 5 sets of numbers in 10 to 15 seconds and slowly increase giving more numbers in the same time.

1	2	3	4	5	6	7	8	9	10
90	60	80	70	66	56	29	84	96	27
- 09	- 01	- 01	- 04	- 11	58	66	43	68	65
- 08	- 10	- 09	- 03	- 04	- 20	49	91	36	35
- 05	- 06	- 08	- 05	- 10	- 11	- 05	- 17	- 20	77
- 06	- 05	- 04	- 20	- 02	- 05	- 09	- 50	- 60	- 60
- 22	- 08	- 10	- 08	- 09	- 18	- 08	- 11	- 30	- 20
- 04	- 02	- 08	- 07	- 07	- 30	- 05	- 06	- 07	- 10
- 03	- 04	- 03	- 09	- 03	- 04	- 20	- 05	- 05	- 30
- 05	- 03	- 05	- 05	- 06	- 02	- 70	- 01	- 08	- 70
- 08	- 03	- 04	- 09	- 05	- 14	- 08	- 40	- 01	- 05

17:S:11

1	2	3	4	5	6	7	8	9	10
25	23	86	46	59	77	37	22	95	56
46	45	17	57	51	31	90	33	11	- 12
39	67	97	64	- 30	48	16	22	- 30	60
54	89	- 10	39	20	- 11	- 05	11	15	07
- 12	10	- 02	- 90	32	60	- 30	55	10	- 40
- 10	- 30	- 80	- 04	- 50	- 40	- 20	- 04	- 20	- 03
25	- 70	- 30	- 10	05	- 11	70	- 09	- 70	02
15	- 40	- 05	- 02	- 70	- 90	70	- 08	09	50
60	- 44	- 05	- 20	- 09	- 14	- 08	- 03	80	90
- 50	- 50	- 50	- 03	- 08	70	- 80	- 20	- 60	01

17:S:12

WEEK 18 – SPEED DICTATION

Goal with speed dictation is to be able to increase the speed of child's calculating skill. Start with dictating 5 sets of numbers in 10 to 15 seconds and slowly increase giving more numbers in the same time.

1	2	3	4	5	6	7	8	9	10
80	42	79	61	67	83	75	29	95	37
- 05	45	21	- 02	- 40	- 04	45	75	15	37
- 06	- 09	- 30	51	80	- 09	- 09	- 03	- 01	24
03	32	- 09	- 90	03	- 01	- 07	- 10	- 09	- 40
- 08	- 08	- 08	88	- 50	50	- 50	- 02	- 60	- 40
06	- 10	- 13	- 04	- 01	01	- 04	- 55	- 06	90
- 02	- 05	- 07	- 14	60	- 40	90	70	50	- 08
- 06	- 04	12	- 03	- 09	- 03	- 06	- 20	- 40	- 20
- 02	- 04	- 03	25	- 09	- 22	- 30	- 04	60	- 08
- 07	- 55	- 40	- 52	- 80	- 22	- 70	- 80	- 04	- 30

18:S:4

1	2	3	4	5	6	7	8	9	10
55	49	64	42	83	46	66	38	85	25
- 11	11	36	42	22	56	- 33	64	92	64
60	50	55	60	- 70	96	44	- 20	- 44	11
07	- 01	- 22	- 50	- 04	- 80	- 22	- 40	- 03	- 40
- 09	- 20	- 05	20	79	- 08	- 11	60	- 07	- 06
- 10	05	- 08	- 40	- 08	- 08	55	30	- 20	90
20	90	- 01	- 40	- 60	- 80	10	- 03	- 50	09
- 30	- 04	- 30	05	- 05	- 05	- 09	- 08	- 10	- 20
- 04	- 03	- 55	- 09	- 07	- 04	- 60	- 07	- 05	- 11
- 08	- 77	- 33	- 01	- 05	- 13	- 06	- 70	- 30	- 40

18:S:5

SAI Speed Math Academy

WEEK 19 – SPEED DICTATION

> Goal with speed dictation is to be able to increase the speed of child's calculating skill. Start with dictating 5 sets of numbers in 10 to 15 seconds and slowly increase giving more numbers in the same time.

1	2	3	4	5	6	7	8	9	10
56	71	29	16	54	19	97	69	24	31
45	43	73	67	52	17	65	29	48	17
53	52	48	72	56	13	65	85	86	79
- 10	- 02	- 01	- 11	- 70	96	- 07	- 40	62	93
- 09	- 05	- 05	- 22	10	- 07	- 07	- 07	- 70	- 06
- 20	- 10	- 09	- 30	- 80	- 80	- 09	- 03	- 06	- 08
- 40	- 09	- 06	- 03	- 04	- 08	- 80	- 04	- 11	- 20
15	- 60	- 40	- 40	33	- 09	- 70	- 20	- 33	- 50
- 40	- 01	01	- 04	- 07	- 06	- 10	- 20	- 10	- 70
- 07	- 02	- 90	- 41	- 09	- 01	55	- 80	- 02	- 11

19:S:1

1	2	3	4	5	6	7	8	9	10
61	48	17	91	24	98	75	34	25	87
27	29	79	37	19	68	49	46	58	31
49	90	93	46	68	19	81	67	45	29
83	86	31	28	37	43	49	79	56	35
- 50	- 10	- 20	- 10	- 90	- 20	- 02	- 50	- 30	- 07
- 06	- 90	- 40	- 40	- 04	- 30	- 05	- 70	- 20	- 05
- 09	- 09	- 01	- 08	50	- 08	- 06	- 10	- 02	- 01
- 07	- 08	- 55	- 06	- 20	- 06	- 06	- 01	- 06	- 50
- 80	- 70	- 90	- 60	- 06	- 07	- 08	- 06	- 70	- 60
- 60	- 66	- 06	- 08	- 40	- 80	- 50	- 30	- 50	- 06

19:S:2

WEEK 20 – SPEED DICTATION

Goal with speed dictation is to be able to increase the speed of child's calculating skill. Start with dictating 5 sets of numbers in 10 to 15 seconds and slowly increase giving more numbers in the same time.

1	2	3	4	5	6	7	8	9	10
16	43	24	43	37	85	59	64	99	81
67	64	52	94	34	16	55	82	05	19
64	49	62	67	36	93	45	19	96	47
56	54	28	16	98	11	45	37	- 10	54
- 30	- 20	- 09	- 20	- 10	- 03	- 60	- 50	- 20	- 70
- 70	- 01	- 30	- 50	- 05	- 80	- 08	- 10	- 40	- 06
- 40	- 09	- 07	- 02	- 06	- 70	- 04	- 70	- 09	- 30
- 08	- 80	- 70	- 08	- 08	- 10	- 80	- 08	- 40	- 02
- 11	- 40	- 09	- 05	- 50	- 09	- 05	- 09	- 06	- 07
- 44	- 05	- 02	- 90	- 60	- 07	- 07	- 50	- 05	- 60

20:S:1

1	2	3	4	5	6	7	8	9	10
37	65	58	95	46	37	27	48	52	63
29	94	73	17	55	16	71	17	83	35
56	19	47	53	86	56	19	38	65	15
79	88	55	36	17	41	83	98	44	37
- 50	- 22	- 06	- 01	- 60	- 05	- 50	- 30	- 80	- 02
- 06	- 90	- 80	- 50	- 05	- 04	- 05	- 04	- 07	- 07
- 90	- 06	- 90	- 09	- 06	- 06	- 10	- 20	- 07	- 06
- 01	- 05	- 03	- 07	- 08	- 80	- 04	- 60	- 70	- 40
- 08	- 04	- 07	- 80	- 30	- 06	- 70	- 03	- 20	- 40
- 07	- 70	- 40	- 06	- 05	- 40	- 60	- 20	- 01	- 11

20:S:2

WEEK 21 – SPEED DICTATION

Goal with speed dictation is to be able to increase the speed of child's calculating skill. Start with dictating 5 sets of numbers in 10 to 15 seconds and slowly increase giving more numbers in the same time.

1	2	3	4	5	6	7	8	9	10
43	52	43	54	66	73	25	15	54	98
12	85	82	- 18	59	35	46	88	49	57
65	25	41	34	- 18	- 24	94	64	18	29
48	- 18	- 60	- 59	- 49	- 06	- 16	- 37	- 06	- 44
- 05	- 29	- 48	64	82	45	- 18	- 26	- 51	- 22
- 06	- 43	51	- 08	- 63	45	- 17	- 14	39	- 33
- 10	58	- 31	51	57	19	- 04	- 05	- 13	- 11
- 40	27	- 24	- 96	- 09	- 53	59	19	- 24	55
- 05	- 12	- 09	24	- 11	- 15	73	- 53	- 26	- 03
- 11	- 15	- 18	- 44	- 13	- 27	- 86	- 16	- 27	- 12

21:S:1

1	2	3	4	5	6	7	8	9	10
53	72	65	58	53	54	24	99	66	37
61	81	- 44	47	57	96	84	04	68	44
48	42	96	- 15	37	- 38	31	- 52	- 27	92
- 54	- 19	- 35	- 14	- 43	- 51	- 44	- 18	- 13	- 64
- 01	- 70	- 41	- 16	- 34	- 22	- 16	54	- 07	- 52
87	36	59	77	55	67	- 18	- 36	15	85
- 25	- 08	- 18	85	96	81	99	84	- 22	- 32
- 25	- 42	25	- 22	- 41	- 15	- 12	- 63	34	43
- 07	- 23	- 03	- 12	- 13	- 28	94	- 14	- 59	- 35
- 63	- 65	51	- 29	- 17	- 16	- 83	- 16	- 55	- 36

21:S:2

WEEK 22 – SPEED DICTATION

> Goal with speed dictation is to be able to increase the speed of child's calculating skill. Start with dictating 5 sets of numbers in 10 to 15 seconds and slowly increase giving more numbers in the same time.

1	2	3	4	5	6	7	8	9	10
46	62	69	79	66	56	84	89	46	86
58	64	33	38	98	28	25	16	19	17
61	25	- 02	51	- 14	28	36	- 07	26	- 05
- 46	- 59	- 02	- 26	59	- 34	- 27	- 53	- 54	95
- 53	- 61	13	- 46	- 24	- 39	- 08	61	93	- 16
- 09	94	- 50	10	- 17	97	83	41	- 10	- 31
32	- 26	- 15	- 54	- 05	- 15	- 46	- 19	- 15	- 28
91	- 15	58	- 17	56	- 24	- 43	22	- 04	33
- 34	- 15	- 14	- 18	14	- 38	- 09	- 11	- 06	- 55
- 47	- 42	- 46	- 17	- 39	67	15	- 59	- 49	- 96

22:S:1

1	2	3	4	5	6	7	8	9	10
55	45	38	63	98	16	99	58	98	74
- 22	58	91	42	14	94	11	63	- 46	42
73	- 09	- 44	18	27	- 55	- 22	- 41	54	36
- 46	95	- 29	- 07	- 94	79	- 33	- 08	- 29	- 44
- 29	- 26	65	- 19	52	52	55	74	76	- 05
82	- 31	76	84	- 14	- 24	- 44	- 17	- 54	99
72	- 35	- 35	52	67	- 56	89	- 26	38	78
- 14	- 78	- 44	- 45	- 84	- 07	- 34	- 07	- 54	- 34
- 79	31	- 38	- 89	38	05	- 23	55	21	- 43
- 32	- 15	- 32	- 52	- 19	- 08	- 29	- 42	- 59	- 19

22:S:2

Dear Parents and Teachers,

We have come to the end of this level. By now, students should be able to comfortably calculate two digit numbers on abacus and in mind. Most students will show a good understanding of the concepts and will also be able to attain good speed and accuracy.

As parents and teachers, you will be able to better judge the knowledge level of your student. If you feel your student needs more practice before taking the 'End of Level' test, you may choose to make your own worksheets for your students or go to www.abacus-math.com and utilize the free worksheet generator to build and print worksheets for your students.

When you generate worksheets from the above website, please choose the values for the criterias as given in the picture.

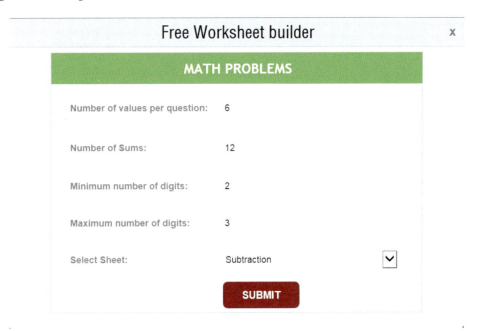

Once students are fluent working with the worksheets, then you may choose to increase the values for the criteria and print more challenging work.

You can let them take the End of Level test given in the LEVEL 3 – WORKBOOK 2 when your student is ready.

Good Luck with the test!

Thank you,
SAI Speed Math Academy

ANSWER KEY

WEEK 2

1	2	3	4	5	6	7	8	9	10	
01	04	20	14	19	12	07	36	03	34	2:S:1

1	2	3	4	5	6	7	8	9	10	
43	22	06	13	12	14	77	90	212	210	2:S:2

1	2	3	4	5	6	7	8	9	10	
13	02	20	64	02	13	12	227	103	332	2:S:3

WEEK 3

1	2	3	4	5	6	7	8	9	10	
55	05	25	25	15	15	33	45	34	135	3:S:1

1	2	3	4	5	6	7	8	9	10	
44	34	28	36	45	350	356	435	55	445	3:S:2

1	2	3	4	5	6	7	8	9	10	
75	46	16	109	35	05	35	35	145	145	3:S:3

1	2	3	4	5	6	7	8	9	10	
05	03	05	00	07	06	04	01	04	03	3:S:4

1	2	3	4	5	6	7	8	9	10	
30	00	90	30	30	40	20	10	80	60	3:S:5

WEEK 4

1	2	3	4	5	6	7	8	9	10	
02	04	23	09	21	14	09	37	24	41	4:S:1

1	2	3	4	5	6	7	8	9	10	
20	38	09	27	52	23	02	103	131	184	4:S:2

1	2	3	4	5	6	7	8	9	10	
33	105	13	123	108	26	101	117	134	321	4:S:3

1	2	3	4	5	6	7	8	9	10	
77	00	55	55	22	33	88	00	00	99	4:S:4

1	2	3	4	5	6	7	8	9	10	
99	44	88	77	55	33	44	55	33	11	4:S:5

WEEK 5

1	2	3	4	5	6	7	8	9	10	
54	08	38	16	26	50	36	06	56	37	5:S:1

1	2	3	4	5	6	7	8	9	10	
46	47	28	35	36	350	66	246	436	446	5:S:2

1	2	3	4	5	6	7	8	9	10	
36	106	136	46	15	06	18	45	466	446	5:S:3

1	2	3	4	5	6	7	8	9	10	
16	45	34	22	66	45	96	24	13	38	5:S:4

1	2	3	4	5	6	7	8	9	10	
30	90	69	99	67	46	40	64	25	14	5:S:5

WEEK 6

1	2	3	4	5	6	7	8	9	10	
15	22	30	60	93	41	50	51	71	67	6:S:1

1	2	3	4	5	6	7	8	9	10	
24	45	40	15	15	07	85	58	76	15	6:S:2

WEEK 7

1	2	3	4	5	6	7	8	9	10	
13	21	03	133	14	03	64	13	54	24	7:S:1

1	2	3	4	5	6	7	8	9	10	
30	33	33	23	33	130	63	114	179	313	7:S:2

1	2	3	4	5	6	7	8	9	10	
55	131	33	45	110	40	04	40	265	128	7:S:3

1	2	3	4	5	6	7	8	9	10	
64	04	24	86	51	30	10	81	09	85	7:S:4

1	2	3	4	5	6	7	8	9	10	
50	57	14	50	23	67	84	03	62	02	7:S:5

SAI Speed Math Academy

WEEK 8

1	2	3	4	5	6	7	8	9	10	
17	29	57	36	18	55	137	67	257	159	8:S:1

1	2	3	4	5	6	7	8	9	10	
37	36	38	46	29	416	477	149	347	447	8:S:2

1	2	3	4	5	6	7	8	9	10	
32	44	44	126	45	44	120	245	245	326	8:S:3

1	2	3	4	5	6	7	8	9	10	
05	83	37	53	15	36	44	96	01	60	8:S:4

1	2	3	4	5	6	7	8	9	10	
70	70	99	60	11	45	40	58	14	01	8:S:5

WEEK 9

1	2	3	4	5	6	7	8	9	10	
41	47	30	30	45	30	27	45	40	20	9:S:1

1	2	3	4	5	6	7	8	9	10	
300	150	270	300	130	310	230	340	310	350	9:S:2

WEEK 10

1	2	3	4	5	6	7	8	9	10	
04	13	34	13	40	09	34	14	39	09	10:S:1

1	2	3	4	5	6	7	8	9	10	
40	90	40	40	39	180	84	119	90	289	10:S:2

1	2	3	4	5	6	7	8	9	10	
139	50	35	31	85	125	24	134	334	247	10:S:3

1	2	3	4	5	6	7	8	9	10	
43	39	30	35	29	30	22	31	33	30	10:S:4

1	2	3	4	5	6	7	8	9	10	
400	250	320	340	290	410	220	450	420	380	10:S:5

WEEK 11

1	2	3	4	5	6	7	8	9	10	
86	30	02	18	17	39	115	58	236	137	11:S:1

1	2	3	4	5	6	7	8	9	10	
42	38	31	48	49	475	348	249	161	486	11:S:2

1	2	3	4	5	6	7	8	9	10	
138	100	115	14	40	33	47	146	281	148	11:S:3

1	2	3	4	5	6	7	8	9	10	
75	65	83	61	50	73	68	61	40	43	11:S:4

1	2	3	4	5	6	7	8	9	10	
247	201	251	255	219	220	297	243	215	182	11:S:5

WEEK 12

1	2	3	4	5	6	7	8	9	10	
17	21	35	38	09	60	25	135	35	139	12:S:1

1	2	3	4	5	6	7	8	9	10	
21	22	13	49	45	46	106	19	346	345	12:S:2

1	2	3	4	5	6	7	8	9	10	
87	26	187	55	28	100	48	149	49	80	12:S:3

1	2	3	4	5	6	7	8	9	10	
74	58	59	42	64	60	53	64	90	62	12:S:4

1	2	3	4	5	6	7	8	9	10	
254	230	137	264	217	207	207	139	305	155	12:S:5

WEEK 13

1	2	3	4	5	6	7	8	9	10	
17	12	34	38	12	66	60	112	136	143	13:S:1

1	2	3	4	5	6	7	8	9	10	
46	33	47	46	47	47	347	448	146	346	13:S:2

1	2	3	4	5	6	7	8	9	10	
79	15	39	44	43	91	27	21	23	44	13:S:3

WEEK 13

1	2	3	4	5	6	7	8	9	10	
288	120	114	232	250	202	225	271	209	292	13:S:4

1	2	3	4	5	6	7	8	9	10	
210	170	236	227	112	200	189	260	211	360	13:S:5

WEEK 14

1	2	3	4	5	6	7	8	9	10	
29	28	29	71	09	81	54	207	202	337	14:S:1

1	2	3	4	5	6	7	8	9	10	
34	47	27	49	100	148	69	137	484	447	14:S:2

1	2	3	4	5	6	7	8	9	10	
10	47	81	33	79	29	83	47	214	206	14:S:3

1	2	3	4	5	6	7	8	9	10	
159	305	314	313	262	302	209	230	202	379	14:S:4

1	2	3	4	5	6	7	8	9	10	
350	301	315	328	230	140	318	363	446	300	14:S:5

WEEK 15

1	2	3	4	5	6	7	8	9	10	
39	58	29	59	16	88	100	138	86	389	15:S:1

1	2	3	4	5	6	7	8	9	10	
38	48	50	49	100	28	49	268	248	501	15:S:2

1	2	3	4	5	6	7	8	9	10	
02	138	48	84	54	115	102	449	74	84	15:S:3

1	2	3	4	5	6	7	8	9	10	
340	340	301	432	280	310	280	400	439	350	15:S:4

1	2	3	4	5	6	7	8	9	10	
300	243	210	282	200	233	212	265	223	210	15:S:5

WEEK 16

1	2	3	4	5	6	7	8	9	10	
43	39	09	39	09	89	98	/99	93	279	16:S:1

1	2	3	4	5	6	7	8	9	10	
59	49	100	49	100	249	49	449	439	449	16:S:2

WEEK 16

1	2	3	4	5	6	7	8	9	10	
100	64	19	39	198	200	46	00	54	293	16:S:3

1	2	3	4	5	6	7	8	9	10	
352	285	410	355	333	261	410	411	253	353	16:S:4

1	2	3	4	5	6	7	8	9	10	
349	396	310	307	220	304	305	321	406	402	16:S:5

WEEK 17

1	2	3	4	5	6	7	8	9	10	
99	98	97	96	95	94	93	92	91	94	17:S:1

1	2	3	4	5	6	7	8	9	10	
95	96	95	97	96	95	98	97	96	95	17:S:2

1	2	3	4	5	6	7	8	9	10	
499	498	497	496	496	494	493	492	499	498	17:S:3

1	2	3	4	5	6	7	8	9	10	
495	496	495	497	496	495	498	497	496	495	17:S:4

1	2	3	4	5	6	7	8	9	10	
90	89	99	99	90	88	98	98	90	87	17:S:5

1	2	3	4	5	6	7	8	9	10	
97	97	90	86	96	96	90	85	95	95	17:S:6

1	2	3	4	5	6	7	8	9	10	
90	84	94	94	90	83	93	93	90	82	17:S:7

1	2	3	4	5	6	7	8	9	10	
92	92	90	81	91	91	105	85	95	95	17:S:8

1	2	3	4	5	6	7	8	9	10	
495	106	85	96	95	496	106	87	95	97	16:S:9

1	2	3	4	5	6	7	8	9	10	
496	107	88	96	95	95	499	499	499	499	17:S:10

SAI Speed Math Academy

WEEK 17

1	2	3	4	5	6	7	8	9	10	
20	18	28	00	09	10	19	88	69	09	17:S:11

1	2	3	4	5	6	7	8	9	10	
192	00	18	77	00	120	140	99	40	211	17:S:12

WEEK 18

1	2	3	4	5	6	7	8	9	10	
53	24	02	60	21	33	34	00	100	42	18:S:4

1	2	3	4	5	6	7	8	9	10	
70	100	01	29	25	00	34	44	08	82	18:S:5

WEEK 19

1	2	3	4	5	6	7	8	9	10	
43	77	00	04	35	34	99	09	88	55	19:S:1

1	2	3	4	5	6	7	8	9	10	
08	00	08	70	38	77	177	59	06	53	19:S:2

WEEK 20

1	2	3	4	5	6	7	8	9	10	
00	55	39	45	66	26	40	05	70	26	20:S:1

1	2	3	4	5	6	7	8	9	10	
39	69	07	48	90	09	01	64	59	44	20:S:2

WEEK 21

1	2	3	4	5	6	7	8	9	10	
91	130	27	02	101	92	156	35	13	114	21:S:1

1	2	3	4	5	6	7	8	9	10	
74	04	155	159	150	128	159	42	00	82	21:S:2

WEEK 22

1	2	3	4	5	6	7	8	9	10	
99	27	44	00	194	126	110	80	46	00	22:S:1

1	2	3	4	5	6	7	8	9	10	
60	35	48	47	85	96	69	109	45	184	22:S:2

ABOUT SAI SPEED MATH ACADEMY

One subject that is very important for success in this world, along with being able to read and write, is the knowledge of numbers. Math is one subject which requires proficiency from anyone who wants to achieve something in life. A strong foundation and a basic understanding of math is a must to mastering higher levels of math.

We, the family, best friends, and parents of children in elementary school, early on discovered that what our children were learning at school was not enough for them to master the basics of math. Teachers at school, with the resources they had, did the best they could. But, as parents, we had to do more to help them understand the relationship between numbers and basic functions of adding, subtracting, multiplying and dividing. Also, what made us cringe is the fact that our children's attitude towards more complex math was to say, "Oh, we are allowed to use a calculator in class". This did not sit well with us. Even though we did not have a specific system that we followed, each of us could do basic calculations in our minds without looking for a calculator. So, this made us want to do more for our children.

We started to look into the various methods that were available in the marketplace to help our children understand basic math and reduce their dependency on calculators. We came across soroban, a wonderful calculating tool from Japan. Soroban perfectly fits with the base-10 number system used at present and provides a systematic method to follow while calculating in one's mind.

This convinced us and within a short time we were able to work with fluency on the tool. The next step was to introduce it to our children, which we thought was going to be an easy task. It, however, was not. It was next to impossible to find the resources or the curriculum to help us introduce the tool in the correct order. Teaching all the concepts in one sitting and expecting children to apply them to the set of problems we gave them only made them push away the tool in frustration.

However, help comes to those who ask, and to those who are willing to work to achieve their goals. We came across a soroban teacher who helped us by giving us ideas and an outline of how soroban should be introduced. But, we still needed an actual worksheet to give our children to practice on. That is when we decided to come up with practice worksheets of our own design for our kids.

Slowly and steadily, practicing with the worksheets that we developed, our children started to get the idea and loved what they could do with a soroban. Soon we realized that they were better with mind math than we were.

Today, 6 years later, all our kids have completed their soroban training and are reaping the benefits of the hard work that they did over the years.

Now, although very happy, we were humbled at the number of requests we got from parents who wanted to know more about our curriculum. We had no way to share our new knowledge with them.

Now, through the introduction of our instruction book and workbooks, that has changed. We want to share everything we know with all the dedicated parents who are interested in teaching soroban to their children. This is our humble attempt to bring a systematic instruction manual and corresponding workbook to help introduce your children to soroban.

What started as a project to help our kids has grown over the years and we are fortunate to say that a number of children have benefitted learning with the same curriculum that we developed for our children.

Thank you for choosing our system to enhance your children's mathematical skills.

We love working on soroban and hope you do too!

List of SAI Speed Math Academy Publications

LEVEL – 1

Abacus Mind Math Instruction Book Level – 1: Step by Step Guide to Excel at Mind Math with Soroban, a Japanese Abacus
ISBN-13: 978-1941589007

Abacus Mind Math Level – 1 Workbook 1 of 2: Excel at Mind Math with Soroban, a Japanese Abacus
ISBN-13: 978-1941589014

Abacus Mind Math Level – 1 Workbook 2 of 2: Excel at Mind Math with Soroban, a Japanese Abacus
ISBN-13: 978-1941589021

LEVEL – 2

Abacus Mind Math Instruction Book Level – 2: Step by Step Guide to Excel at Mind Math with Soroban, a Japanese Abacus
ISBN-13: 978-1941589038

Abacus Mind Math Level – 2 Workbook 1 of 2: Excel at Mind Math with Soroban, a Japanese Abacus
ISBN-13: 978-1941589045

Abacus Mind Math Level – 2 Workbook 2 of 2: Excel at Mind Math with Soroban, a Japanese Abacus
ISBN-13: 978-1941589052

LEVEL – 3

Abacus Mind Math Instruction Book Level – 3: Step by Step Guide to Excel at Mind Math with Soroban, a Japanese Abacus
ISBN-13: 9781941589069

Abacus Mind Math Level – 3 Workbook 1 of 2: Excel at Mind Math with Soroban, a Japanese Abacus
ISBN-13: 9781941589076

Abacus Mind Math Level – 3 Workbook 2 of 2: Excel at Mind Math with Soroban, a Japanese Abacus
ISBN-13: 9781941589083

Made in the USA
Coppell, TX
05 March 2020